THE GREAT EXCHANGE: YOUR THOUGHTS FOR GOD'S THOUGHTS

RENOVATING YOUR MIND WITH GOD'S WORD

By Robb Thompson

It is a privilege for me to write this endorsement for Robb Thompson's book, *The Great Exchange: Your Thoughts for God's Thoughts*. I have personally known Robb Thompson for more than a decade. He is not only a fellow minister, but my personal friend and a member of the Board of Directors for Rick Renner Ministries.

Because I know Robb well, I can promise you that the message he conveys to you in this book is not just theoretical; it is an overflow of what God has done in his own life. These are principles and truths that emphatically *are* accessible to and doable for every believer who chooses to renew his or her mind with the Word of God. And I personally know of no better example to prove the validity of these truths than the life of Robb Thompson himself.

As you read this book, I advise you to apply its life-changing and practical principles to the way you think and speak. If you'll do that, I guarantee that you'll experience a "great exchange" as you begin to think the thoughts of God and see every situation of life in a brand-new way!

Rick Renner
Rick Renner Ministries
Apostle to the former Soviet Union

The Great Exchange: Your Thoughts for God's Thoughts is a powerful yet simple book that teaches you how to experience a daily transformation by grasping the truth of what God has already done for you in Christ. Robb Thompson walks you through this process of change using his own testimony of the renovating power of God's Word to change even the most difficult struggles of the mind and personality.

Pastor Mark Hankins
In Christ Ministries
Alexandria, Louisiana

Pastor Robb Thompson is a man of integrity with a pastor's heart. In this book, he stresses that you must renew your mind if you desire to experience victory in your life. *The Great Exchange: Your Thoughts for God's Thoughts* is a message from Robb's heart that will help you do just that.

Pastor Stan Moore
Words of Life Fellowship Church
Miami, Florida

In *The Great Exchange: Your Thoughts for God's Thoughts,* Robb Thompson has developed "vitamins for the mind." Each chapter is a mega-dose that detoxifies the mind! This is the single best "stress-buster" I've ever read. Do you want *relief*? Just read this book today! Robb Thompson's story is living proof that the Holy Spirit and the Word of God are the best counselors!

Pastor Dewey Friedel
Shore Christian Center
Allenwood, New Jersey

The Great Exchange: Your Thoughts for God's Thoughts Renovating Your Mind With God's Word
ISBN 1-889723-20-7
Copyright © 2001 by Robb Thompson
Family Harvest Church
18500 92nd Ave.
Tinley Park, Illinois 60477

Editorial Consultant: Cynthia Hansen
Text Design: Lisa Simpson
Cover Design: Greg Lane

DEDICATION

I dedicate this book to the multitudes of those in Christianity who struggle between their old life and their new identity in Christ. These same brothers and sisters are tossed by every wind of doctrine. May this small book be the doorway of discovery to all they have been made in Him.

Én Agape,
Robb Thompson

TABLE OF CONTENTS

ACKNOWLEDGMENTS

I want to acknowledge several people for their great contributions in making it possible for me to put this book in print.

First and foremost, I would like to thank the Holy Spirit, for without His teaching and patience during the learning process, I would not be qualified to speak these words.

I would like to thank my wife Linda. Without her consistent encouragement and persistence in doing things right, I may have never continued to follow God.

I also want to thank Dave Scherer. Without Dave's commitment to the Word of God and his unending example of believing God, I would not have changed.

I would like to thank Kenneth and Gloria Copeland for being such great examples of people who held on to the Word of God until it transformed them.

I also would like to thank my assistant, Tina Spada. Without her diligence and commitment, this book would not have gone to press.

Finally, I want to thank my editor, Cindy Hansen, for dedicating her time to helping me put this message on paper.

For these people I am forever grateful.

Robb Thompson

FOREWORD

Finally, here's a book that gives us insight and practical teaching concerning the workings of our carnal brain and our renewed mind! In *The Great Exchange: Your Thoughts for God's Thoughts*, Robb Thompson explains in detail how the process of renewing the mind works.

Personally, I believe that you cannot conquer yourself until you conquer your mind. That's why I believe this book is a must for your Christian library. If you want to succeed in life and have what the Word says you can have, you have to realize the importance of your thought life.

Robb stresses that there is a difference between *conforming* and *transforming* because conforming requires us to make changes on the *outside*, whereas being transformed is something that begins on the *inside*. Robb is right! The world is always trying to change us from the outside, but the root of every problem lies within. That's why the Word of God is so important!

In this book, Robb encourages you to truly believe in your inner transformation — to live *in Christ*, refusing to allow the devil to steal your confidence in God's work in your life through negative thoughts.

Robb explains that the Bible isn't a self-help book to get you on the road to changing yourself from the outside. It is a Book filled with spiritual, life-giving words that will transform you into a new creature. As Second Corinthians 5:17 (*KJV*) says, **"Therefore if any man be in Christ, he is a new creature: old things are passed away; behold, all things are become new."**

I really enjoyed this book. As you read it, I believe it will change your thinking on a lot of subjects in the Bible. You may ask, "Why would it do that?" I'll tell you why! It will get your carnal brain thinking like a renewed mind! Robb will show you how to rid yourself of mental pressure so you can start thinking with a "saved brain."

You'll like this book. I liked it! And I believe Jesus likes it, too, because the principles in this book will draw you closer to Him, which is just what He wants! What more could you ask for?

So are you ready to let the old things pass away? Are you ready to uncover "the new you"? Then get yourself a cup of coffee and a doughnut, and find a place to relax. It's time to read this book! *Let the renovation begin!*

Jesse Duplantis

INTRODUCTION

The human mind is one of the most intriguing and complex aspects of God's entire creation. In fact, the more we find out about the mind, the more we realize how little we know! The mind has been used to accomplish the greatest achievements in man's history. It has also been used to destroy, demean, and degrade, bringing countless people to their knees through a perverted form of its power.

Through the centuries, multitudes of Christians have allowed the enemy to use their minds to destroy not only their own lives, but the lives of those around them. You see, the mind is the arena where battles are won or lost; nevertheless, it has always been one of the most misunderstood areas of Christianity.

Despite the complexities of the mental realm, the bottom line is this: Man's mind was meant to be controlled by the Word of God. If a person can gain control of his mind with God's Word, he will be able to win in every area of life.

Whoever controls your mind controls your life. It's as simple as that. With that in mind, I want to share some scriptural principles with you that are absolutely vital in helping to bring God's will to pass in your life. These principles will map out the path you must follow in order to acquire what I call "saved brains" — in other words, a renewed mind that thinks the way God thinks *all* the time and not just on Sundays.

The starting point of this journey begins with one basic truth — that the intake of Bible doctrine is the most important thing in your life as a believer. *Nothing* can take the place of your commitment to continually feed on God's Word.

That's why I have nothing for you outside of what God has to say on this subject of the mind — or any other subject, for that matter. I'm not interested in religion. I'm not interested in little pet doctrines that people pick up along the way. I am only interested in that which *God* has written. If you can show me a truth in the Word of God, I'll act on it. If I don't see it in the Word, I'm not interested in doing anything about it.

Now, let me assure you that I haven't just developed a nice little theoretical teaching on this subject of renewing the mind. I've had to apply these principles to my life on a daily basis for my own spiritual survival!

You see, this is a subject that comes from the very depths of me. I was saved in 1975 while being treated in a mental institution. The doctors told me there was nothing they could do for me. They helped me through the toughest part of what they called a "deep character disorder" and then informed me I would be that way for the rest of my life. But the power of God's

Word delivered me! In fact, one hundred percent of the deliverance I have enjoyed has been through the application of the scriptural principles I'm about to share with you.

God has already given you everything you could ever need in life to achieve victory over an unrenewed, defeated mind. But how are you going to bring that victory into your practical experience? Just how do you accomplish "mind renovation"? That, my friend, is the exact question I'm going to answer for you in this book. So let's get started on the scriptural path that will lead us to our goal: accomplishing "the great exchange" — your thoughts for God's thoughts!

Robb Thompson

C H A P T E R

FROM CONFORMED
TO TRANSFORMED

If you're a believer, I have some astounding news for you. You don't have to wait for God to set you free because *you are already free.* Jesus has already done all He's ever going to do to deliver you from every demonic bondage, bad habit, or mental stronghold you could ever face.

So how do you live in the freedom that is already yours? Jesus gives you a vital key in John 8:31,32: **"...If you abide in My word, you are My disciples indeed. And you shall know the truth, and the truth shall make you free."**

You see, right now you stand on the launching pad of life. God's Word already dwells within you. But it is as you *continue* in the Word that you receive the fuel you need to catapult into God's divine blessings and live in the freedom that already belongs to you. And it all begins as you start obeying Romans 12:2: **"And do not be CONFORMED to this world, but be TRANSFORMED by the renewing of your mind...."**

The Purpose Behind Renewing the Mind

First, let's take a closer look at that passage of Scripture in Romans 12. It will help you get a better idea of why it's so important to begin this process of renewing, or renovating, your mind.

> **I beseech you therefore, brethren, by the mercies of God, that you present your bodies a living sacrifice, holy, acceptable to God, which is your reasonable service.**
>
> **And do not be conformed to this world, but be transformed by the renewing of your mind, that you may prove what is that good and acceptable and perfect will of God.**
>
> **Romans 12:1,2**

The word "beseech" in verse 1 is an interesting term. On one hand, this word refers to an admonishment that brings correction. On the other hand, it also refers to an encouragement or exhortation. So Paul was actually saying, "I'm both correcting and encouraging you, brethren...."

This phrase "I beseech you therefore, brethren" was used by a Roman military commander when he addressed his troops right before going forth into battle. The commander's goal at that time was to encourage his troops and get them excited about gaining the victory. He knew that in every battle, there is always an opportunity to lose. The soldiers never knew whether they would return from the next battle.

Therefore, the commander encouraged his men by reminding them of what they needed to do to win the fight. To that same end, he also had his soldiers constantly training, day in and day out. Even when they were not in battle, they continued to practice doing the very things they'd be required to do on the battlefield.

In the same way, you and I have the opportunity to lose the good fight of faith. How could we lose? Either by refusing to train for war or by giving up in the midst of the battle.

That makes Paul's next phrase in verse 1 very important to us: **"I beseech you therefore, brethren, BY THE MERCIES OF GOD...."** In the midst of divine correction and encouragement, we run smack dab into the love of God!

Paul is referring to God's great compassion for us. We once were in a horrible, miserable state of need. (I know that was certainly true of me!) But God's mercy and compassion arose and came upon us in the midst of our great need. He said to us, "I love you. I'll take care of you. I'll watch over you. I'll do it all for you. You just need to relax and let Me take care of this situation."

So in essence, Paul is saying this: "I'm admonishing and encouraging you as if you were going out into battle because, in reality, you live in the midst of a spiritual battle every day of the week. You wake up to a battle each and every morning. You cannot escape being confronted with Satan's tactics on a daily basis. In fact, the day you're free from that kind of spiritual battle is the day you go home to be with the Lord!

"However, the good news is that 1) you never have to be ignorant of the enemy's devices, and 2) you never have to lose, because God's love always leads you into victory. It is by God's love that you are encouraged to fight this fight of faith. God's love is something you can trust and believe in. His love will never let you down."

Paul goes on to say in verse 1 (*NAS*):

...Present your bodies a living and holy sacrifice, acceptable to God, which is your spiritual service of worship.

In light of our miserable state of need, God now tells us what to do in order to honor His mercy and compassion. We are to present our bodies to Him as living sacrifices.

That means you are not to have the spiritual backbone of a wet noodle, allowing every carnal thought that passes through to set up residence in your mind. Instead, you are to yield your body and your mind as a sacrifice unto the Lord, which the Bible says is your reasonable service of worship.

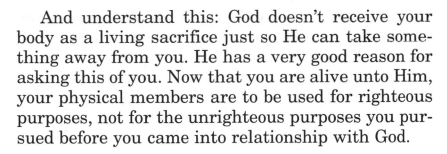

And understand this: God doesn't receive your body as a living sacrifice just so He can take something away from you. He has a very good reason for asking this of you. Now that you are alive unto Him, your physical members are to be used for righteous purposes, not for the unrighteous purposes you pursued before you came into relationship with God.

That's why Paul then says:

And do not be conformed to this world, but be transformed by the renewing of your mind....

That word "conformed" refers to being *formed* or *molded*. We are not to be molded or conformed to the "shape" of this world. In other words, we are never to imitate or adopt the way this world does things. We're not to be moldable to the circumstances that are happening in our lives. We are to be moldable only to God and His Word.

As we mold ourselves to God's Word, we are *transformed* by the renewing of our minds. In using this word "transformed," Paul is talking about a profound change that takes place within our innermost being.

You see, *conforming* requires a person to make changes on the outside, but being *transformed* is something that happens on the inside of a person. Christians usually live their lives in a backward fashion. They usually try to fix who they are on the *outside*, all the while thinking that somehow God is going to bless who they are on the *inside*.

But it doesn't work that way. The spiritual lives of these Christians gradually become hollow and lifeless. Why? Because they're trying to change something in their own natural strength that can only be changed through an inner transformation.

As you continually look into the Word of God for your answers to every situation of life, the Word will change the way you think. It will change the way you live. It will change everything about you. And there is no other way for that inner transformation to take place. It comes only through the renewing of your mind by God's Word. This explains why God told Joshua:

> **"This Book of the Law shall not depart from your mouth, but you shall meditate in it day and night, that you may observe to do according to all that is written in it. For then you will make your way prosperous, and then you will have good success."**
>
> **Joshua 1:8**

Ephesians 5:25 confirms this truth when it says Jesus cleanses the Church with the washing of water by the Word of God. It is only by supernatural "washing" that Jesus is able to **"...present her to Himself a glorious church, not having spot or wrinkle or any such thing, but that she should be holy and without blemish"** (Eph. 5:27).

The word "renew" carries a similar idea to this supernatural "washing." God's Word continually washes and renews your mind as you feed on it continually. The more you allow the Word of God to permeate your mind and heart — the more you think about what it says and speak it with your mouth — the more it completely transforms you from the inside out.

That word "renewing" also carries the idea of turning around, as with a revolving door. You are transformed by turning the thoughts of God around in your mind day after day. As your mind becomes a revolving door for God's thoughts, sooner or later it will be completely conformed or molded to think the way God thinks. This is essentially what it means to renew your mind.

Now, the term "mind" in Romans 12:2 refers to your way of thinking and the power of your reasoning ability. You are to be transformed by the changing of your reasoning ability, or, as the apostle Paul put it, **"...renewed in the spirit of your mind"** (Eph. 4:23). You are no longer to reason according to the reasoning of this world. Instead, you are to use the reasoning abilities God has given you to think the way *He* thinks.

For instance, look at what God says in Isaiah 1:18:

> **"Come now, and let us reason together,"**
> **says the Lord, "Though your sins are like**
> **scarlet, they shall be as white as snow;**
> **though they are red like crimson, they**
> **shall be as wool."**

Even though you think your sins are horrible, God says you are as white as snow. Although you may think you're red like crimson, God says you're like pure wool. You see, when you reason with God, you always come out on top!

Isaiah 55:8-11 tells us that through His Word, God always gives us one of His higher thoughts to replace every carnal thought that might come to our minds. He never leaves us without an answer.

"For My thoughts are not your thoughts, nor are your ways My ways," says the Lord.
"For as the heavens are higher than the earth, so are My ways higher than your ways, and My thoughts than your thoughts.
"For as the rain comes down, and the snow from heaven, and do not return there, but water the earth, and make it bring forth and bud, that it may give seed to the sower and bread to the eater,
So shall My word be that goes forth from My mouth; it shall not return to Me void, but it shall accomplish what I please, and it shall prosper in the thing for which I sent it."

I no longer want to reason according to the old carnal thought patterns of my past. I am not interested in the wrong thoughts that might run through my mind today. I am only interested in what God's Word says.

Only when my mind coincides with God's Word do I accept what it says. I do not believe my mind unless I can show myself and everyone around me that it lines up with what God has to say on the matter. You see, I know my mind lies to me at times. I also know I'm not an isolated case. If my mind lies to me, yours just might lie to you too!

Finally, Romans 12:2 tells us the primary purpose for renewing our minds: that we may prove, or demonstrate, what is the good and acceptable and perfect will of God.

These three words — good, acceptable, and perfect — are not three levels of God's will for your life; rather, they are three adjectives that describe what God's will is to you. It's good; it's acceptable; and it's perfect for you. And as you are transformed by the renewing of your mind, you will demonstrate in your life what it means to enjoy the good, acceptable, and perfect will of God!

The Starting Place For Conquering Your Mind

Now, that doesn't mean you'll just skyrocket overnight into the higher realms of victory in Jesus. That isn't even God's desire for you. He knows you wouldn't be able to live in a position you too quickly attained.

You see, the spiritual life is a life of growth. Living in victory is something you grow into. That's true in any area of life, but especially in this area of renewing the mind.

Therefore, God stresses again and again that we are to meditate on the Word, confess the Word, and spend regular, quality time in the Word. Why? Because that's how we grow in our spiritual walk. We have to conquer our carnal minds in order to experience the freedom that already belongs to us.

"Conquering your mind" means you must bring your mind under subjection to God's Word until it is unmoved and unaffected by the world's thinking and anything that concerns evil. The starting place for this process lies in believing Second Corinthians 5:17 (*KJV*):

Therefore if any man be in Christ, he is a new creature: old things are passed away; behold, all things are become new.

You know, it never seems to fail. Whenever people come to me for help, their problem is based on something that happened in the past or something that was true about them before they were born again. These people may not realize it, but they are actually contradicting God's promise to them that old things have passed away in their lives. They will never be able to do themselves or anyone else any good until they come to truly believe they have been translated out of Satan's dark realm into God's Kingdom of light and victory.

Let's look at a couple key phrases in this important verse. First, Paul states that if we are in Christ, we are "new creatures." This is a term that the Jews understood. When a Jew talked about a person being a new creature, he meant that the person's sins were forgiven and that God was able to account unto him righteousness because he believed.

Now notice that phrase "old things are passed away." Let me use this analogy to help you better understand what this means. Think of what the horizon looks like when a storm front is moving through your area. You might see the front coming from as far as one hundred miles away. You watch as the wind blows the dark clouds closer and closer. And when the front finally arrives on the scene, it brings a big change to your surroundings! Lightning flashes, thunder crashes, the wind whips the tree branches, and the rain pounds the ground as the front rolls through.

But as the front moves on, you can look up in the sky and see an end to the dark clouds. That lets you know that in just a short time, the thunderstorm will pass away. The rain will stop, and the sun will break through the clouds.

Think of all the negative things that wreaked havoc in your life before you received Jesus as your Savior — the sinful habits, the wrong associations, the carnal thought patterns, the demonic strongholds. Start seeing all those negative things as a part of the "old things" that have "passed away," just like a storm front that moves through your area, leaving bright sunshine in its stead.

Old things have passed us by. When we received Jesus Christ as the Lord of our lives, we became new creatures. Those old sinful habits and carnal thought patterns that absolutely ran our lives before we were born again no longer have any right to rule and reign! Now the light of the Son has come to shine inside our lives. We don't have to live under dark clouds of oppression and defeat anymore!

How I Began To Learn About Mind Renovation

I know from personal experience how important it is to let the revelation of Second Corinthians 5:17 replace your "stinking thinking." You see, if my life had just gone according to the course of natural events, I never would have been able to live even a nominal Christian life. I would have backslidden many moons ago had it not been for the renewing of my mind.

As I said earlier, I got saved in a mental institution in 1975. One of the things that put me in that mental institution was the devil's strategy to keep beating on my mind. He'd use a particular series of thoughts to keep talking to me and talking to me and talking to me and talking to me, trying to break me down so I'd accept his lies as truth and commit all kinds of sinful acts. Over and over he'd say to my mind, *You want to do this; you want to do this; you know you want to do this..."*

Then one day it all came to a head as I was riding home from work. (I owned a downtown business that imported audio equipment from England and Japan.) I was getting off the highway at my exit when suddenly all the subconscious fears I'd ever had came rushing to the forefront of my mind.

As long as these fears stayed on the backside of my mind, I could still function and look like I was having a great time in life. Once in a while one or two of these fears would surface, and I'd be depressed for a while. But I always just denied the reality of those tormenting thoughts and pushed them far enough into the background to keep on going about my daily routine.

However, that all changed in one moment of time as I was driving down the exit ramp. Suddenly *all* those subconscious fears became a part of my conscious thoughts. I couldn't shoot them in the back anymore. I couldn't say, "Oh, no, that's not real. I'm not really depressed."

I felt like I had been ambushed. With the ferocity of machine gun bullets, my hidden fears bombarded my mind. My heart started beating 250 miles a second. I did everything I knew to do to get rid of the frantic thoughts racing through my mind, but they wouldn't go away. I felt totally lost.

This didn't fit the image I projected to the world at all. Man, I was *cool,* and cool guys didn't go through this kind of mental torture. Cool guys didn't go nuts!

Meanwhile, the devil kept talking and talking and talking to my mind: *You want to do this. You want to do this. You want to do this. You want to do this. You want to do this. You want to do this. You want to do this. You want to do this. You want to do this!*

Finally, I started thinking, *Do I? Do I really want to do this? I guess I really want to do this. I guess I just need to go try it and find out.* Suddenly that demonic thought had me agreeing with it!

But something inside me still fought back. I thought, *NO, NO, NO, NO!*

Yes, you want it.

No, I don't!

Yes, you do.

No, I don't!

YES, YOU DO!

From that moment on, I was constantly fighting against this intense mental bombardment. It took a heavy toll on me. For three months, I ate only when I had to and slept only when I was exhausted. Twice I tried unsuccessfully to kill myself.

Finally, I ended up in the mental institution. I felt safe in that place behind heavy, locked doors. I couldn't get out, but no one else could come in and get me either. As long as I was behind those locked doors, I felt like everything would be fine.

Then one day a man came and told me that I could know Jesus and that Jesus would change my life. I told him, "I don't want to know about God." But deep inside, I knew there was something different about this fellow. What that difference was, I really didn't know. But I knew he had something in his life that I didn't have in mine.

So I started making sarcastic remarks to this Christian man to see if I could "push his buttons" and make him upset with me. I tried, but he didn't go for it. He just kept talking to me about Jesus.

So I told him, "I think I'm going to Heaven."

"Why?" he asked.

"Because I'm a nice guy. Actually, I'm a very nice guy, if I do say so myself."

The man said, "That isn't good enough." Then he told me about Jesus dying for the sins of the world. He said Jesus died for me personally so I could be born again. Then he explained what that meant. By receiving Jesus as my Savior, I could have a new life; everything about me could become brand new.

I said, "Okay, so what do I have to do?"

He said, "You don't have to do anything but pray."

"I can do that," I replied. So this man led me in prayer, and I received Jesus as the Lord of my life on October 28, 1975.

Before the man left, he gave me his Bible, but that was it. He didn't give me any coaching on how to live this new life I had just received. So I slept with my Bible, thinking that would do something for me. Amazingly, it seemed to work! The next morning I woke up knowing I was a brand-new person. All the mental pressure that had been relentlessly pushing me and attempting to destroy my life had suddenly disappeared.

Jesus had invaded my life, and everything was great for months. Then one day those terrible thoughts started coming back again, and I didn't know what to do with them. You see, I didn't know I had a new set of rules and standards, so I fell into the trap of trying to fix myself.

You're probably familiar with this "self-help" way of thinking: *Well, I'm a Christian now, and I need to figure out how to get rid of the problems I have in my life.* That was how I understood the Christian walk. I thought, *Robb, there's something wrong with you, or you wouldn't be thinking those thoughts. You need to straighten yourself out!*

The devil started beating on my mind again with those same thoughts: *You want to do this. You want to do this. You want to do this. You want to do this.* Every day I'd get a migraine headache from the mental pressure. Every day I'd go into my closet to cry and repent because, even though I didn't want to sin, I just couldn't seem to stop it. I'd beg God to be free, but it only got worse.

I thought my life was over. After all, now I was a Christian, but I was still thinking those ungodly thoughts. I thought that once a person became a Christian, he didn't have problems anymore!

Then came the day I first learned about renewing the mind. I was sitting in a restaurant reading the Bible. As I sat there reading, this thought suddenly occurred to me: *When am I really going to believe that I am a new creature? When am I going to come to the place where I believe that what the Word of God says about me is true?*

Right then I made a decision to believe the Bible, no matter what. The day I made that decision was the day my life turned around. Before that, the devil could beat me up in my mind anytime he wanted to. But that day I began to replace the devil's thoughts with *God's* thoughts, and that put me on the road to freedom!

Don't Claim Those Thoughts as *Yours*!

You see, Satan cannot destroy your life until he first confuses your identity. He cannot destroy you until he can get you to believe that the problem is you.

As long as you believe that the wrong thoughts running through your mind are *your* thoughts, you will never be free and you can never succeed. All the devil has to do is sow one lying thought in your mind to make you a failure. You will think that thought is your own and accept the devil's lie that you're a horribly wicked person.

But that is absolutely not true! That's why it's so important to understand this truth: The thoughts in your mind that are contrary to God's Word are *not* your thoughts.

How do I know that? First of all, Proverbs 12:5 says, **"The thoughts of the righteous are right...."** If you have received Jesus Christ as the Lord of your life, you are righteous, my friend. Righteousness doesn't depend on your actions; it depends on what Jesus did for you through His death, burial, and resurrection. After all, if you could get to Heaven by being good, why did Jesus have to die for your sins?

You are righteous in Christ, so the thoughts you have are only right. If thoughts come to your mind that are not right thoughts, they are not your thoughts.

"Yes, but I'm the one thinking those thoughts!" you might say. No, those wrong thoughts are just passing through.

When you got born again, you were born of incorruptible seed, which is the Word of God.

> **Since you have purified your souls in obeying the truth through the Spirit in sincere love of the brethren, love one another fervently with a pure heart,**
> **having been born again, not of corruptible seed but incorruptible, through the word of God which lives and abides forever.**
>
> **1 Peter 1:22,23**

At the moment of salvation, you became a new creature. Old things passed away, and you received a new life. As Jesus said in John 15:3, **"You are already clean because of the word which I have spoken to you."** That word "clean" has to do with being morally pure, sinless, and unstained.

However, the Bible never talks about your mind being saved. It just says your mind has to be *renewed*. You see, there are two things that didn't get saved when you did: 1) your mind, and 2) your body.

Therefore, your mind isn't really who you are. You don't have to feel condemned about thinking wrong thoughts. You can just tell yourself, *Well, that thought didn't come from me anyway, so it's nothing for me to worry about. Just move on out, lying thought! I'm morally pure, sinless, and unstained by the blood of Jesus and the Word that has been spoken to me!*

Many of us really have no idea what is happening when our thoughts seem to go awry. We think there's something wrong with us. We think that somehow we have suddenly become carnal and that our spiritual walk falls far short of what it should be.

You may be thinking right now, *Oh, God, what am I going to do? No one understands the thoughts I've been thinking.*

But I do understand, because the devil tells everyone the same thing. He isn't telling you one thing and telling me another. The way he tells you that he's going to kill you is the same way he tells me. The way he says you're going crazy is the same way he tells me. The way he accuses you of being carnal or having wrong desires is the same way he accuses me.

So what makes the difference in the outcome of people's lives when the devil uses the same lies for everyone? *The difference rests in the fact that one person believes his lies, and the other one doesn't.*

How do you react to the wrong thoughts that run through your mind? Do you receive those thoughts, or do you reject them?

My friend, you can't believe every spirit. That's why First John 4:1,2 says this:

> **Beloved, do not believe every spirit, but test the spirits, whether they are of God; because many false prophets have gone out into the world.**
> **By this you know the Spirit of God: Every spirit that confesses that Jesus Christ has come in the flesh is of God.**

We know from verse 2 that *spirits communicate with words.* Jesus said in John 6:63:

> **"It is the Spirit who gives life; the flesh profits nothing. The words that I speak to you are spirit, and they are life."**

The words that are spoken to us are spirit. That's why God said, **"Beloved, do not believe every spirit...."** Don't believe every word that comes into your mind. Don't think that every time negative words come into your mind, those wrong thoughts are from you. Remember, my friend, you are righteous in Christ, and the thoughts of the righteous are only right!

Therefore, reject sharply any thought that doesn't coincide with Jesus coming in the flesh or with what God's Word says about you. Command it to leave your mind. Say, "No, you can't stay here. You must leave me now!"

That's so much better than spending all your time thinking, *You don't know what I'm going through. I feel so bad.* If you allow yourself to receive all the devil's horrible thoughts, you won't go anywhere but down in defeat. In fact, until you can come to the place where you believe God's Word above the thoughts that run through your mind, you're not even at ground level!

The devil knows if he can get you to believe the thoughts that come to you, all he has to do is wait until you start feeling discouraged. Then he'll start bombarding you with all sorts of abominable thoughts. It won't be long before you don't even think you're a Christian anymore!

Someone might ask you, "Are you saved?

"I just don't know anymore!" you'll moan in despair.

Think about it, friend. If you couldn't get to Heaven by being good, why would you go to hell by doing something bad? I mean, you didn't get saved because you thought a bunch of good thoughts. So how can you get *un*saved by thinking a bunch of bad ones? You can't! *Besides, those wrong thoughts are not even your thoughts in the first place!*

The Desires of Your Heart
Are Only Good

Proverbs 11:23 gives us more scriptural proof to support this statement. It says, **"The desire of the righteous is only good...."** So the desires that come from down on the inside of you are actually desires that originate in God. That's why Jesus could say in Mark 11:24:

"Therefore I say to you, whatever things you ask when you pray, believe that you receive them, and you will have them."

Let me explain to you one application of this scripture where it says, **"Therefore I say to you, whatever things you ask when you pray...."** During your time of prayer and communion with God, a desire may suddenly hit your heart that you never thought of before. If behind that desire you sense a "yes!" deep down on the inside of you, it's safe to assume God has just planted that desire in you because **"the desire of the righteous is only good...."**

This goes along with Second Corinthians 5:18 (*NAS*), which says, **"Now all these things are from God...."** What things is the apostle Paul talking about? He tells us in verse 17 (*NAS*): **"...the old things passed away; behold, new things have come."**

Paul is saying that every attribute down on the inside of you right now is of God. Old things have passed away, and new things have come. Therefore, you can know this beyond a shadow of a doubt: Every wrong thought that violates God's Word is not yours to claim — it is the enemy's to reject!

You Have *Everything* Pertaining
To Life and Godliness

Second Peter 1:3,4 also has something to say about this:

...His divine power has given to us all things that pertain to life and godliness, through the knowledge of Him who called us by glory and virtue,
by which have been given to us exceedingly great and precious promises, that through these you may be partakers of the divine nature, having escaped the corruption that is in the world through lust.

Through the Lord's glory and goodness, He has placed into your charge all things that pertain to life and godliness. He's given you all the physical and material blessings you could ever need. By His grace, God has also given you all the spiritual equipment you need to be like Him in every area of life. However, whether or not you enjoy the benefits God has given you is determined by whether or not you *believe* in those benefits.

Then verse 3 says that you have been given God's very great and precious promises so that by those promises you may become a partaker of His divine nature. Those same promises enable you to escape the corrupt lusts of the world and the pressures of carnal desire that try to bombard your mind and hinder your walk with God.

We all know there is a great deal of pressure in this world. Every day we go through one type of pressure or another, whether it's financial, physical, mental, or spiritual. Sometimes the pressure becomes so great that we feel like either giving up or isolating ourselves from the rest of the world while we hang around with our little circle of Christian friends.

God has given His promises to us to provide a way of escape from all that pressure. However, that divine escape is found only *through His Word*.

Now, one problem many Christians have is that they use the Word of God to *fulfill* their pressures rather than to *escape* them. Let me tell you what I mean by that statement.

The pressure to pay bills is something every one of us goes through every month. But the Word of God was given to us to escape the pressure of having to pay the phone bill, the electric bill, and every other bill that stares us in the face.

For instance, when the phone bill comes, we may think, *What am I going to do? Lord, I'm asking You for the money to pay my phone bill.*

But that isn't escaping pressure. In fact, that's actually fulfilling pressure rather than escaping it! To escape the pressure of that phone bill, we have to remind ourselves that God's Word has given us everything pertaining to life and godliness. Absolutely everything! This would have to include enough money to pay the phone bill because that is a need pertaining to life on this earth.

So what is our escape in regard to the phone bill? We believe the Word of God, which says Jesus became poor so we could become rich.

For you know the grace of our Lord Jesus Christ, that though He was rich, yet for your sakes He became poor, that you through His poverty might become rich.

2 Corinthians 8:9

The Bible also says if we will meet the needs of others, God will meet our needs.

Now you Philippians know also that in the beginning of the gospel, when I departed from Macedonia, no church shared with me concerning giving and receiving but you only....
And my God shall supply all your need according to His riches in glory by Christ Jesus.

Philippians 4:15,19

Since God is going to take care of us, we don't need to worry about the phone bill or any other pressure in our lives.

So always remember — everything pertaining to life and godliness is resident within your recreated human spirit. Your needs are already met. Your prayers are already answered. Everything in life you could ever desire already belongs to you and is already down on the inside of you.

Therefore, let it always be said about you that you are eagerly awaiting the manifestation of God's Word in your life. With the confidence born of faith in what God says about you, you reject any thought that contradicts the Word and refuse to claim it as your own. You have made your choice to be transformed by the renewing of your mind. Therefore, every thought, every word, every action, and every circumstance in your life must bow its knee to what is written!

2

IDENTIFIED WITH JESUS

If I had to pick one aspect of the Christian walk in which I am personally the strongest, it would be the understanding of what it means to be identified with the Lord Jesus Christ and how to experience the benefits of that identification in my everyday life. This understanding is the very basis for knowing which thoughts to believe and which to reject when they come into my mind.

Identifying with Jesus also keeps me from allowing things that have happened in my life to hinder my present or to hamper my future. I do not live one moment of my life in guilt. I don't waste time wishing I had done something else with my life. I don't go around fretting to myself, *Robb, you're thinking all these negative thoughts, so there must be something wrong with you.* The only thing that ever bothers me when negative thoughts go through my mind is that I don't yet fully understand how those thoughts slip in.

I'm looking for the answer to that question. How do wrong thoughts slip into my mind so swiftly and with such strength? I don't even know how they got there; I certainly didn't invite them in. Nevertheless, one thing I've learned over the years is that *we can't determine who knocks on our door, but we CAN determine whom we let in!*

Too many times we open the door as soon as the devil knocks, giving him access to our minds so he can torment us regarding different areas in our lives. This torment can actually rule us and press us into becoming someone we don't want to be. That's why I've made it a point over the years to learn how to stop inviting wrong thoughts to come into my mind. I don't want to give the enemy license to torment me and hamper my life.

I want to share with you what I've learned on this topic of identification. Gaining an understanding of what it means to be identified with Christ is crucial if you want to renovate your mind as the Bible commands.

Our Twofold Identification

The word "identification" actually means *to treat as being the same*. It comes from the same base word as "identical," which means *to look the same*. So if we are identified with Christ, we look the same as Christ.

This teaching of identification is the legal side of our redemption. Romans 5:1,2 tells us that our ability to identify with Jesus in His redemptive work has been given to us by the grace of God.

Therefore, having been justified by faith, we have peace with God through our Lord Jesus Christ,
through whom also we have access by faith into this grace in which we stand, and rejoice in hope of the glory of God.

When we identify with Christ, we come to understand what He accomplished through His death, burial, resurrection, and ascension on High, where He now sits at the right hand of the Father. This then causes us to experience everything Jesus experienced.

What do I mean by that? Well, as First Corinthians 6:17 says, **"...he who is joined to the Lord is one spirit with Him."** So through identification, you come to realize that you are one with Christ in every aspect of His redemptive work. You died with Christ; you were buried with Christ; you suffered with Christ; you were made alive with Christ; and you are now seated with Christ in heavenly places.

The prepositional phrase "with Him" in this context actually gives us the key to understanding our identification with the Lord Jesus. It also gives us the key to understanding exactly what happened to us when we were born again.

We are one spirit *with* Jesus. This oneness or this identification we have with Christ is twofold. First, we were identified with Christ on the Cross. Second, we have been raised and are now seated with Him on His throne.

Ephesians 2:1,4-6 (*KJV*) talks about this twofold identification:

And you hath he quickened, who were dead in trespasses and sins;...

But God, who is rich in mercy, for his great love wherewith he loved us,

Even when we were dead in sins, hath quickened us together with Christ, (by grace ye are saved;)

And hath raised us up together, and made us sit together in heavenly places in Christ Jesus.

Verse 1 (*KJV*) says, **"And you hath he quickened...."** That term "quickened" just means "And you hath he *made alive*." You once were spiritually dead in your trespasses and sins; you didn't have any of God's life on the inside of you. But even while you were still dead in your sin, God made you alive by His Spirit, quickening you together with Christ (v. 5).

Verse 5 (*KJV*) goes on to say, **"...(by grace ye are saved;)."** Once again, we see that it was God's grace that enabled us to identify with Jesus' death and resurrection through the new birth.

The first half of identification has to do with you and I being judged with Christ. Romans 4:25 says that Jesus **"...was delivered up because of our offenses, and was raised because of our justification."** Jesus didn't go to the grave because of anything He had done; He never committed one sin while He was on this earth. He went there because of what *we* had done.

Therefore, Second Corinthians 5:14 (*KJV*) says this:

For the love of Christ constraineth us; because we thus judge, that if one died for all, then were all dead.

The word "constraineth" in this verse means Jesus' love drives us to make a decision. That decision is based on His love, demonstrated through His death on the Cross, and it causes us to realize this truth: When this One died for all, His death was our death.

Jesus died for you. That means two things: 1) you were once dead in your sins, and 2) you died with Him. So the first step in knowing you are identified with Christ is to identify with Him in His death. When Jesus died, you died. When Jesus was buried, you were buried. When Jesus was in the tomb, you were in the tomb.

But when Jesus died for you, He didn't leave you in the grave. Sure, you died and were buried with Jesus when you became a believer, but you aren't supposed to *stay* inside the grave. Now you have to come out of the grave and enjoy your new life in Him!

Therefore, the next step is to identify with Jesus in His resurrection life. When Jesus was raised, you were raised together with Him. When Jesus was seated in heavenly places, you were seated right next to Him. That may sound simple, but many Christians never understand these two steps of identification. And, sadly, if they don't stop always looking at *who they are not*, they can never truly know in practical experience *who they are in Christ*.

What It Means To Be Baptized Into Jesus' Death

Romans 6:1-6 (*KJV*) tells us more about these two steps of identification:

What shall we say then? Shall we continue in sin, that grace may abound?

God forbid. How shall we, that are dead to sin, live any longer therein?

Know ye not, that so many of us as were baptized into Jesus Christ were baptized into his death?

Therefore we are buried with him by baptism into death: that like as Christ was raised up from the dead by the glory of the Father, even so we also should walk in newness of life.

For if we have been planted together in the likeness of his death, we shall be also in the likeness of his resurrection:

Knowing this, that our old man is crucified with him, that the body of sin might be destroyed, that henceforth we should not serve sin.

This passage of Scripture contains some very important truths for us. Paul asks, "Shall we continue to sin so that grace may abound? Then he almost screams, *"God forbid!"* Since we are dead to sin, it should be unthinkable to us to live any longer as servants of sin.

Then in verse 3, Paul asks, **"Or do you not know that as many of us as were baptized into Christ Jesus were baptized into His death?"** We were immersed into Jesus' death when we were born again. Therefore, we were buried with Him by baptism into death.

Now, this verse isn't talking about water baptism. One particular denomination interprets the verse that way; thus, members of that denomination claim that a person's water baptism is what makes him part of the family of God.

But that just isn't true. This verse is speaking about the spiritual baptism or immersion you experience when you first believe in Jesus Christ, not about your baptism in water *after* getting saved.

Understand this: You don't gain anything just because you've been dunked in water. The water you're baptized in doesn't have any special power in it. It does no more for you spiritually than your bath water does for you when you take a bath!

Water baptism is just an *outward* manifestation of something that has already happened to you *inwardly*. First Peter 3:21,22 puts it this way:

> **There is also an antitype which now saves us — baptism (not the removal of the filth of the flesh, but the answer of a good conscience toward God), through the resurrection of Jesus Christ,**
> **who has gone into heaven and is at the right hand of God, angels and authorities and powers having been made subject to Him.**

The truly important points to understand about water baptism are these:

- When you were baptized into Christ spiritually, you were baptized into His death.

- In the same way Christ was raised from the dead by the glory of the Father, even so you should walk in the newness of life.

You Have To *Know* You Died With Christ

So what does it really mean to say, "I died with Christ"? Romans 6:6 gives us some insight on the matter:

> **Knowing this, that our old man was crucified with Him, that the body of sin might be done away with, that we should no longer be slaves of sin.**

Notice the phrase "knowing this." Whenever the Word of God tells us that we need to know something, we can just assume that we *really* need to know it! Paul is telling us, "Know this. Understand this. Keep your mind on this." What are we to know? **"...that our old self was crucified with Him...."** (v. 6 *NAS*).

So when my old self is giving me problems and "jumping my case," trying to get me to go in the carnal direction it wants me to go, that's the time to remind myself of what I already know — that my old self was crucified with Christ. And if my old self was crucified with Him, my old self can't make me do anything!

When people talk to me about going back to the life they had before they were born again, I say to them, "Let me ask you something — are you a believer?"

"Yes, I am," they say, "but you just don't know what I'm going through. You just don't know the kind of pressure I've been feeling to do some of the wrong things I used to do. I don't want to do them, but the devil keeps *telling* me I want to do them."

I reply, "That's why it's so important to know that your old self was crucified with Jesus. But you have to understand that if your old self was crucified with Him, that doesn't mean you never have to deal with it again. Remember, dying on that Cross was a long, hard, painful process!"

That's why Pilate was so amazed when he found out Jesus was already dead after only three hours on the Cross. A crucifixion was supposed to last for many hours — sometimes for days! Of course, Jesus didn't die on the Cross as just another human being; He became sin for us:

For He made Him who knew no sin TO BE SIN for us, that we might become the righteousness of God in Him.

2 Corinthians 5:21

A human body doesn't live long when the person who lives inside that body actually becomes sin!

Because dying to your old self is such a difficult, painful process, it makes sense that the word "know" in verse 6 is a word denoting progression in a particular direction. You are to continually move *toward* the One whom you seek to know. As you do, you come to truly know and understand that your old self was crucified with Him.

Now, who is your old self? Well, I certainly know what my old self was like. Prior to knowing Jesus, the guy who used to live inside my body constantly did all sorts of wrong things. He embezzled money. He was a thief. He took drugs. He was an alcoholic by the time he was sixteen. He was sexually immoral.

Isn't that a great testimony? No, it isn't! It's a horrible testimony. I'm not proud of it at all. But I *am* proud of what the Word of God has done in me. I have cause every day to think about what my life was like before October 28, 1975. If I chose to, I could dwell on how horrible things used to be and how my flesh always wants to drag me back into my previous state of sin and torment. But I *don't* choose to. I choose to dwell on who *God* says I am in His Word!

Turn the searchlight on your own life, and ask yourself this question: *What do I talk about most of the time?*

Do you spend a lot of your time talking about the terrible things that happened to you before you were saved? Do you focus on all the problems that are going on in your life right now? If these are the things you continually talk about, you really need to examine your spiritual walk. According to the words of your mouth, Jesus must not mean much to you.

What does it really mean to have Jesus in your life? Does it mean you have a cross hanging on the wall of your bedroom and a Bible sitting on the bookshelf? Does it mean you have some nice Christian friends you can call on when you need some help? No! It means your old life has passed away forever. It means you can follow the psalmist's example in Psalm 3:

> **I lay down and slept; I awoke, for the Lord sustained me.**
> **I will not be afraid of ten thousands of people who have set themselves against me all around....**
> **Salvation belongs to the Lord. Your blessing is upon Your people.**
>
> **Psalm 3:5,6,8**

When Jesus is a living reality in your life, this psalmist's words becomes *your* testimony. You can close your eyes at night, knowing that, no matter what you're going through, you will awake in the morning in peace because the Lord sustains you!

How do you get to that place in your spiritual walk? You take that first step of identification we've been talking about. In other words, you come to the place where you *know* deep on the inside that your old self was crucified with Christ.

If you don't know that crucial truth, here's what happens: You receive Jesus as your Savior and throw all your cares on Him because He cares for you. Then Satan shows up and says to your mind, *Come on, don't you want to do all those things you did last week? Wouldn't that be fun?* He begins to put pressure on your physical senses — what you can see, hear, and feel — so you won't spend your time meditating on and believing what God's Word says. He knows your feelings speak louder than your spirit does.

Because you don't know that your old self was crucified with Christ when you were born again, you start believing the devil's thoughts. Finally, you act on those thoughts and begin a downward spiral back into bondage and defeat.

Free From My Past

That's why it's so important to understand this subject of identification. Personally, I believe the reason I haven't been tremendously hindered by my past is this: I understood early in my Christian walk that *the day I got born again was the day I died.* For years I've walked around with Romans 6:6 and Galatians 2:20 in my mouth.

Knowing this, that our old man was crucified with Him, that the body of sin might be done away with, that we should no longer be slaves of sin.

Romans 6:6

"I have been crucified with Christ; it is no longer I who live, but Christ lives in me; and the life which I now live in the flesh I live by faith in the Son of God, who loved me and gave Himself for me."

Galatians 2:20

I confess on a regular basis, "Father, I thank You that I know my old self was crucified with Christ. I am no longer a slave to sin! I have been crucified with Christ, and it is no longer I who live, but Christ lives in me!"

Galatians 2:20 is just as true for you as it is for me. You have been crucified with Christ. It is no longer you who live, but Christ lives in you. So what does that mean in practical experience? Well, does Christ have perverted thoughts? No. Does Christ have defeated thoughts? No. Does Christ have impoverished thoughts? No! Well, then, if it's no longer you who live, who is the source of that "stinking thinking" in your mind? It can't be you because that old self is dead. It must be the enemy of your soul!

Think about it. You can't put cancer on a dead man, can you? You can't put heart trouble on a dead man. You can't put poverty on a dead man. When bills come after someone is deceased, you just write "Deceased" on those bills and send them back. (You might want to try that with your bills today, but it won't work because your creditors can still see your body moving!)

You also can't get a dead man to do something wrong. You can walk up to the coffin and try to convince him to sin, but he isn't going to respond to you in any way, shape, or form. You'll never get an argument out of the guy in the casket. No matter what you try to do to that dead man, he won't react or receive it. He won't receive any more sickness or disease. He won't receive any more poverty. He won't receive any more temptation to sin. No matter what you do, you are not going to change a dead man.

That's how I look at myself. Robb Thompson died on October 28, 1975. From that day forward, his old self no longer existed. However, I can still choose to *make* him exist. How? By continuing to believe that who I was before that day is the real me.

Remember, I got born again in a mental institution. That's where I came to know Jesus. I know what it is to have trouble with your mind. I know what it is to wonder who you are.

When you have six or seven conversations going on in your head at the same time and you're not sure who you are, you start doing some funny things. You start pacing the floors at night. You start walking around the streets like a crazy man.

That's what I did anyway. I'm telling you, the man who used to live in this body before October 28, 1975, was nuts. He had had it. It was over for him.

Physically, I felt like a zombie. I was so tired, I didn't want to talk to anyone.

You see, when a person has all kinds of voices talking to him inside his head, he doesn't feel like talking anymore. For one thing, he doesn't know which one of those voices is actually the one talking in any given conversation. After a while, he starts wondering, *Am I okay?* The answer is simple: "No, you're not! You're crazy!"

Anyway, after I was born again, it took me about a year and a half to get on track and begin renewing my mind. But after that, I never looked back.

People might say to me, "But, Robb, look at all the horrible things you did. Look at how you messed up those people's lives. Look at how you treated this person. Look at all the stuff you stole. Look at all those lives you ruined through drugs, alcohol, and every other perverted thing you got involved with before you came to know Jesus. Do you mean to say that you don't ever look back at all the wrongs you've committed against others in the past?"

That's exactly what I mean.

"But, Robb, haven't you struggled with inner hurts because of the way people treated you in the past or because of the wild things you experienced when Satan was destroying your life? Haven't you carried all those hurts into your new life?"

No, I haven't!

"Well, that may be okay for you, but I just need the Lord to heal me."

Let me tell you something, my friend. You're about as healed as you're ever going to get. I mean, what else can Jesus do for you when He has already erased your old life of sickness, poverty, and defeat? He has already given you a brand-new start. He has already said your old self is dead. Never again do you need to think about that old life you had before you knew Him as your Savior.

You Don't Need More Forgiveness

What more could Jesus do for you? You may say, "Well, I just need to receive more forgiveness." How much more forgiven can you be when God has already separated you from your sins **"as far as the east is from the west..."** (Ps. 103:12 *KJV*)?

Have you ever met someone who has to keep asking forgiveness for the same offense over and over? He asks a person to forgive him, and the person agrees to do so. But then he asks that same person ten more times to forgive him for the same thing: "Oh, can you ever forgive me? Can you ever forgive me?" Finally, the other person starts thinking, *Ai, yi, yi! What's wrong with this guy? I wish he'd just accept the forgiveness I gave him the first time he asked!*

That's probably how God feels about Christians who think it demonstrates holiness and humility to constantly ask Him for forgiveness. In reality, it demonstrates pride in their lives. It's nothing but pride to think that the sins they have committed are greater than the forgiveness Jesus has already provided for them.

You don't truly believe that God loves you if you're still saying in essence, "Jesus, what You've done for me isn't quite enough. I want to make sure I'm *really* forgiven." You have to come to terms with what you really believe. What do you believe more — that you're forgiven, or that you're still filled with your past?

You may answer, "Well, I believe God." Well, then, if you believe God, you have to reject the thoughts that torment you about your past sins and receive the forgiveness He has already given you.

In fact, when you commit a sin, you don't even have to go to God and cry out, "Lord, forgive me!" The Word of God never says that you need to ask God to forgive you. All He ever told you to do was to confess or cite the sin you have committed, and He'd forgive you.

If we confess our sins, He is faithful and just to forgive us our sins and to cleanse us from all unrighteousness.

1 John 1:9

In confessing your sin, you are agreeing with God and condemning the sin He has already passed sentence on. In His eyes, it has already been judged.

God can't give you any more forgiveness than He has already given you. That would mean that the precious blood of Jesus has only intermittent effectiveness, and we know that's not true!

Understanding that we don't need any more forgiveness is a vital part of identifying with Christ's death, and it goes far beyond our own personal need to benefit from its truth. Second Corinthians 5:19 tells us that it is the very message God has commissioned us to tell the world:

...God was in Christ reconciling the world to Himself, not imputing their trespasses to them, and has committed to us the word of reconciliation.

The term "reconciling" just means that God made the world a friend of Himself. Then he committed unto us this word of reconciliation.

In other words, we are to let people know that God has already forgiven them. We aren't supposed to go around telling everyone, "Listen, we need to get you forgiven." They're already forgiven; we just need to help them *believe* it!

Upheld by God's Word

If you want to live your life unhindered by mental torment about past sins and hurts, you have to come to a place in your spiritual walk where you are separated from your old self once and for all. See yourself becoming more one with Jesus than with your problems. Make it your quest to identify with Him, and remember — the trials you go through don't ever have to touch you.

Hebrews 1:3 says that God upholds all things by the Word of His power. Do you want to be upheld? Then get on the Word of God. You're upheld when you keep your mind and heart stayed on the Word. But if you get off God's Word and try to live according to your own reasoning ability, you'll end up drowning in the troubles of life!

You see, God is always going to be there to make sure His Word comes to pass. Look at what Numbers 23:19 says:

"God is not a man, that He should lie, nor a son of man, that He should repent. Has He said, and will He not do? Or has He spoken, and will He not make it good?"

Then in Isaiah 46:10,11 (*AMP*), God confirms this:

"...My counsel shall stand, and I will do all My pleasure and purpose....
Yes, I have spoken, and I will bring it to pass; I have purposed it, and I will do it."

God has never said He would do something and then refused to follow through. He's always faithful to fulfill His Word!

That's why Hebrews 10:23 (*KJV*) says, **"Let us hold fast the profession of our faith without wavering; (for he is faithful that promised;)."** The term "hold fast" is a nautical term. The writer of Hebrews is saying in essence, "Let us tie ourselves to and wrap ourselves around the Word of God like a sailor lashes himself to the mast to keep from being thrown into the stormy sea. Even though our 'faith ship' is being tossed around by the storms of life, we don't ever have to be thrown overboard."

Now notice what we are to hold fast to: **"Let us hold fast the profession** [or confession] **of our faith...."** The phrase "profession of faith" just means *that which agrees with faith and with the Word of God*. Let us tie ourselves around that which agrees with what God says about us, for the One who promised is absolutely faithful!

The problem is, many people don't hold on quite long enough. They start listening to the devil's thoughts in their minds and become deceived. They start thinking, *God, all the things You say about me in the Bible can't be real. I don't think I'll ever change.* Finally, they lose heart and let go of their confession of faith, speaking forth the words of defeat and discouragement that have taken up residence in their minds.

Separated by the Cross

One of the most important truths you could ever hold fast to is this: *It is the Cross of Christ that separates you from your old life.* In Galatians 6:14, Paul puts it this way:

But God forbid that I should boast except in the cross of our Lord Jesus Christ, by whom the world has been crucified to me, and I to the world.

Often when I see people crying out to the Lord, pleading with Him to move on their behalf, I want to ask them, "Why are you doing that? Why are you spending all your time on your face before God, crying out for Him to do something for you? Jesus has already done absolutely everything He is ever going to do for you."

When Jesus said from the Cross, "It is finished," that's exactly what He meant. Everything He needed to do for mankind is already finished. It's over. Jesus is now sitting at the right hand of the throne of God. He's done with His redemptive work!

Jesus has already spoiled principalities and powers. He's already forgiven you. He's already put all your enemies under your feet. He's already done everything the Father has asked Him to do. Every spiritual blessing has already been deposited for you in Heaven:

Blessed be the God and Father of our Lord Jesus Christ, who has blessed us with every spiritual blessing in the heavenly places in Christ.

Ephesians 1:3

In fact, Hebrews 2:8 says, **"...For in that He put ALL in subjection under him, He left NOTHING that is not put under him...."**

Everything is under Jesus' feet. That means if I'm part of the Body of Christ — even if I'm a wart on the bottom of Jesus' foot — everything is underneath *me*.

First John 3:8 explains why this is true:

> ...**For this purpose the Son of God was manifested, that He might destroy the works of the devil.**

The very reason Jesus was manifested was to destroy, to annihilate, to bring to nothing, and to paralyze the works of the enemy in your life. There isn't one work of the enemy against you that hasn't already been destroyed!

Think back to Second Corinthians 5:17 (*NAS*):

> **Therefore if any man is in Christ, he is a new creature; the old things passed away; behold, new things have come.**

The *New Living Translation* says it this way:

> **What this means is that those who become Christians become new persons. They are not the same anymore, for the old life is gone. A NEW LIFE HAS BEGUN!**[1]

The day you were born again was the day your life began. You don't ever need to think about what happened to you before that day. You don't need to wonder about what's going to happen to you next

---

[1] *Life Application Study Bible; New Living Translation* (Wheaton; Illinois; Tyndale House Publishers, 1996), p. 1840.

week, next month, or next year. You don't ever need to think about your former passions and desires — the things you once wanted to accomplish in life — because now God has a better plan for you.

You may feel the flame when creditors are pulling at you, but you don't have to let that flame burn you because Jesus has already paid your bills. And when the doctor walks in and says, "I'm sorry, but it's almost all over for you," you don't have to sit there and cry because it *isn't* almost all over. Jesus has already paid the price for your healing, and *He* says you're healed!

That's what I mean when I say the Cross of Christ separates us from all that we were before receiving Jesus. Through the Cross, the world has become a dead thing to me, and I have become a dead man to the world. It's no longer I who live, but Christ lives in me. I am a walking dead man. Now I walk through each day with the life of God running through my veins. I cannot go back to my old life and be satisfied any longer. The Cross has separated me from that old life once and for all.

You know, it never works to return to your old life after becoming a believer. You end up more miserable than you ever were before you got born again. Your second condition is worse than the first because now you can't sin without troubling your born-again spirit.

And understand this: Satan cannot legally cause you to go back to what you were before the day you received Jesus. You would have to go back under your own volition. It's a decision only you can make, and that decision has to do with what you believe. Whatever you believe is what you act on. That's why you must believe in the power of Jesus' death and resurrection to separate you forever from the person you were before you were born again.

The negative thoughts that try to pull me and draw me back into this world have become dead to me. It isn't difficult for me to reject them completely whenever they run through my mind because I have now become a dead man to the world. As far as I'm concerned, the pull of this world doesn't exist. I don't want any part of it. I don't really care about it. It doesn't matter to me. I'll do what God tells me to do, no matter what. The only thing that matters to me in life is "What does the Word of God say?" That's it!

I don't know where God's going to take me in life. He is filled with surprises. I'm just going to watch Him work out His plan in my life as I concentrate on staying obedient to Him. And in order to keep my heart constantly turned exactly the way God's heart is turned, I will always stay submitted to that which is written in His Word.

That's the attitude you need to adopt for your own life. Don't boast in anything or anyone except the Cross of the Lord Jesus Christ. Remember, it's that Cross that separates you from your old life. Your old life can't control you anymore. You'll never go back to that old life unless you choose to believe that your old self is who you really are. Don't ever let yourself believe that, because whatever you believe is what you'll bring to pass in your life.

Choose Life!

In Deuteronomy 30:19, God not only tells you that you must choose between life or death, blessing or cursing — He also tells you which one to choose!

I call heaven and earth as witnesses today against you, that I have set before you life and death, blessing and cursing; therefore choose life, that both you and your descendants may live.

God is saying, "Now, I know you're going to go through a test, so I'm going to give you the right answer. *Choose life* so that you and your descendants may live!"

So follow God's wise counsel. Choose to identify with Jesus Christ in His death, burial, resurrection, and ascension on High. Meditate continually on the fact that your old self has been crucified with Jesus. Your old life is gone forever, and your new life has come. As you do that, you will become more and more transformed by the renewing of your mind, and the promise of your future will shine very, very bright!

THE KEY TO VICTORY: UNDERSTANDING RIGHTEOUSNESS

People constantly say to me, "You know, I read the Bible, I pray, I go to church, and I witness to people about the Lord. So why does it seem like whenever 'the pedal meets the metal' and the pressure is on, I resort to my old ways?"

The answer to that question is simple. You haven't yet come to realize whom Jesus has made you and what He has done for you through His death and resurrection. In order to successfully withstand the pressures of this world and renovate your mind according to the new life that is yours in Christ, you must understand righteousness — the ability to live continually in rightstanding with God.

More specifically, the biblical term "righteousness" refers to the ability to stand in God's Presence without the sense of guilt, inferiority or failure, free from accusation, as if sin had never existed. You can easily see why your spiritual success depends on your understanding of this vital subject!

I can safely say that most of the blessings I've experienced in my life have come as a result of understanding my righteousness in Christ. I've seen countless prayers answered and multitudes of people healed and delivered as I have stood fast in faith according to my rightstanding before God.

You see, if you don't understand righteousness, you're in trouble as soon as you go to pray for someone. The devil will tell you, *You ugly thing, you. Look at what you did this afternoon. Why do you have the right to pray for anyone?* When that happens, you have to believe you are righteous in Christ, or your faith will fizzle like a balloon that's just been pricked with a pin!

Living in the New Covenant With an Old Covenant Brain

It's sad to say, but most Christians don't understand righteousness. Instead, they live in the New Covenant with an Old Covenant brain.

What do I mean by that? Well, under the Old Covenant, God wrote His commandments in stone with His finger. He told His people, "Don't commit adultery. Don't bear false witness. Don't have any

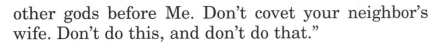

other gods before Me. Don't covet your neighbor's wife. Don't do this, and don't do that."

But the Ten Commandments are *not* the message of the Gospel. Under the New Covenant, we actually become the righteousness of God in Christ. Our lives are governed by the law of love, not by a bunch of "do's and don'ts."

A Christian who doesn't understand his own righteousness before God eventually begins to live his life like a little robot, consumed with his efforts to fulfill all the "do's" and avoid all the "don'ts." But on the inside, his mind is ripping him apart as he struggles with those old, carnal desires to do the things he knows are wrong.

That's what I mean by people who live in the New Covenant with an Old Covenant brain. These people think they can work for or earn something from God. They continually say, "If I do these things, God will be pleased with me."

Friend, that isn't the way it works. The reason you're getting beaten up in life is that you're thinking wrong. You're thinking, *Oh, God, there's something wrong with me! If I could just get this area of my life straightened out, I know You would answer my prayer.*

But that's an absolute, bold-faced lie from the devil! If you could do something in your life in order to receive from God, why did Jesus die for you? If there was anything that anyone could do in order to gain God's favor, why did Jesus have to die for the sins of the world?

"Oh, well, He died for bad people." Well, what about you?

"Well, you know, I'm not so bad." Now you're suddenly comparing yourself with the person next to you. Does that mean the other person is bad and you're not?

Or you may be thinking, *Well, you know, it isn't really bad for me to ask God to meet my needs.* That may be true, but there is still a better way. A blood-bought Christian already has all his needs met. As far as God is concerned, he is healed; he is prosperous; his marriage is blessed; and his kids are obedient to the faith. As a believer, he is abundantly blessed in this life and Heaven-bound for the next life. Everything he could ever need has already been provided. So why does that person think he has to try to get God to do something for him?

When sickness shows up at my house, why would I ask God to heal me when First Peter 2:24 already says that by Jesus' stripes, I *was* healed? If I *was* healed, then I must *be* healed right now! So I don't go before God's throne asking Him to heal me. I go there thanking Him that I *am* healed.

That isn't what the New Testament person with the Old Testament brain does. He thinks there's something he has to convince God to do for him so his needs can be met. He's waiting for God to do something to make him complete. He doesn't know what that "something" is, but he's pretty sure he doesn't have it yet!

There is nothing you need in your life as a believer that you don't already have. That's the message I'm trying to get across to you.

The Gospels —
Still Old Covenant

In order to understand righteousness, it's also important to understand that the people in the Gospels were still under the Old Covenant. The Gospels do not give us New Testament teaching. Jesus walked on this earth as the Son of God and a Prophet under the Old Covenant, fulfilling the Law for us. He did not walk on this earth as a new creature. We can know this is true because of what Paul said in Second Corinthians 5:16: **"...Even though we have known Christ according to the flesh, yet now we know Him thus no longer."**

Now, how did Paul know Jesus after the flesh? He knew Jesus after the flesh because he had heard people talk about Him who had personally known Him. He knew Jesus after the flesh because the authors of the Gospels had already started writing about Him. He knew Jesus as the One who walked the shores of Galilee and who walked up to people and asked, "Sir, would you be made whole?"

Do you realize Jesus wouldn't ask you that question today? Jesus wouldn't come to you and ask, "Well, now, I know you don't really have your healing, so do you want to get healed?" Why wouldn't He do that? Because He knows that by His stripes, you *were* healed. He has already done everything He's going to do to provide healing and health for your body. When that realization hits your heart, you will stop knowing Jesus "after the flesh"!

There came a time when Paul said, "We are not to know Jesus after the flesh any longer." In other words, we must finally realize that there's nothing we can do to receive anything from God. The only thing we can do is believe what He said.

Now let's apply that truth to this subject of righteousness. Let's say I mess up "to the max" one day. (I know you have never done that, so I'll just talk about me!)

Then I pick up my Bible and read Second Corinthians 5:17: **"Therefore, if anyone is in Christ, he is a new creation; old things have passed away; behold, all things have become new."**

A few verses later, I read that **"...He made Him who knew no sin to be sin for us, that we might become the righteousness of God in Him"** (v. 21).

I start thinking to myself, *Boy, if I could just be the righteousness of God!* Then I flip the pages over to James 5:16 (*KJV*) and read, **"...The effectual fervent prayer of a righteous man availeth much."**

I talk to God: *Lord, if I could just be righteous, I'd be a praying dude! If I could just be righteous, I know You'd answer every one of my prayers. You'd be able to use me. You could trust me. You could do all sorts of wonderful things in my life, Lord, if I could just live as a righteous person.*

Well, if you could live as a righteous person in your own strength, why did Jesus have to die for your sins? Let me tell you something — you can't do it!

As a matter of fact, all you have to do is read Isaiah 64:6 to know you can't live righteously on your own:

But we are all like an unclean thing, and all our righteousnesses are like filthy rags; we all fade as a leaf, and our iniquities, like the wind, have taken us away.

Let me talk to you about filthy rags for a minute. This Hebrew term refers to the rags women used for their menstrual cycle. So God was saying that every good thing you might try to do is nothing better than what's left over at the end of a woman's menstrual cycle! The best thing you could ever produce on your own isn't even good enough to be used again. In God's eyes, it's just a filthy rag that is good for nothing but the trash can.

That's why Jesus said, "Truly I'm telling you that a man has to be born again" (*see* John 3:5-7). The only way you can get out of the Gospels and into the New Covenant is to be born again. At the moment of salvation, you became a new creature, the righteousness of God in Christ. You'll never be any more righteous than you were at that moment you first believed.

Recognize Jesus as Your Substitute

What does it really mean to be a "believer," or one who believes in Jesus Christ? Well, number one, you must allow Jesus to be your Substitute. You have to believe that Jesus took your place on the Cross. He died for you so you don't have to die. He became exactly what you were so you could become exactly what He is.

The truth is, if you haven't allowed Jesus to become your Substitute, my friend, then you're not a believer and you are destined for hell.

"But I don't believe Jesus had to suffer for me." Well, if Jesus didn't have to suffer for you, you can be sure that *you're* going to suffer because one way or another, sin must be judged.

Isaiah 53:4 talks about the substitutionary work of Jesus Christ:

> **Surely He has borne our griefs and carried our sorrows; yet we esteemed Him stricken, smitten by God, and afflicted.**

Because of the stand Jesus took, the Jews actually thought God had cursed Him. And, really, that's exactly what happened. God did curse Jesus for our sake.

Now let's look at the next two verses:

But He was wounded for our transgressions, He was bruised for our iniquities; the chastisement for our peace was upon Him, and by His stripes we are healed.

All we like sheep have gone astray; we have turned, every one, to his own way; and the Lord has laid on Him the iniquity of us all.

Isaiah 53:5,6

Jesus actually died for us. In Romans 5:8, it says, **"But God demonstrates His own love toward us, in that while we were still sinners, Christ died for us."** Long before you ever thought of drawing near to Jesus, He said, "I'm making the commitment to die for you so you don't have to die."

We should always remind ourselves that a divine exchange was made for us on the Cross — one Man's righteous life for our unrighteous lives. Jesus exchanged His righteousness for our sin. That's why Second Corinthians 5:21 (*KJV*) says, **"For he hath made him to be sin for us...."**

Jesus was made to be sin. Notice it doesn't say He was made to be *sins*. No, God made Jesus to be *the sin nature* for us. Why? Because that's what we were.

For he hath made him to be sin for us, who knew no sin; that we might be made the righteousness of God in him.

2 Corinthians 5:21 (*KJV*)

We traded positions with Jesus. He was righteous and became unrighteous. We were unrighteous and became the righteousness of God as Jesus **"...was delivered up because of our offenses, and was raised because of our justification"** (Rom. 4:25).

Romans 5:1 tells us the result of that divine exchange:

Therefore, having been justified by faith, we have peace with God through our Lord Jesus Christ.

We have God's Word on it: Because Jesus traded His righteousness for our unrighteousness, we now have peace with the God of the universe forevermore!

View Yourself According to the Word

You know, God's Word needs to be your best friend every day and every night. But the Word can speak to you in two ways. It can speak to you positively, or it can condemn you. *You* are the one who makes the choice.

The only difference between the person who believes the Word of God and the person who is condemned by it is the way both individuals view themselves. For instance, the believer who doesn't understand righteousness might look at First Corinthians 6:9,10 and feel condemned by it:

Do you not know that the unrighteous will not inherit the kingdom of God? Do not be deceived. Neither fornicators, nor idolaters, nor adulterers, nor homosexuals, nor sodomites,

nor thieves, nor covetous, nor drunkards, nor revilers, nor extortioners will inherit the kingdom of God.

Have you ever felt "caught" by those verses yourself? I've talked to people like that. They make comments such as, "The Bible says the unrighteous won't inherit the Kingdom of God. But I've done some of those unrighteous things, and so have you!" I just stand there thinking, *No, you're not talking about me. I'm righteous because I believe — not because I do right things.*

Sometimes people get stuck in verses 9 and 10 and never get to verse 11, which says this:

And such were some of you. But you were washed, but you were sanctified, but you were justified in the name of the Lord Jesus and by the Spirit of our God.

I like what the *Amplified* says: **"...but you were washed clean...and made free from the guilt of sin...."** That's how we are to view ourselves. We are those who have been cleansed by the blood of Jesus Christ, no longer judged by our unrighteous acts of the past. In Romans 1:16 and 17 (*KJV*), the apostle Paul explains the supernatural process that has taken place in our lives:

> **For I am not ashamed of the gospel of Christ: for it is the power of God unto salvation to every one that believeth; to the Jew first, and also to the Greek.**
>
> **For therein is the righteousness of God revealed from faith to faith: as it is written, The just shall live by faith.**

The *Lovett* paraphrase of verse 17 says it this way:[2]

> **It** [the Gospel] **reveals God's way of making men as righteous as Himself. It is a process which, from beginning to end, is entirely by faith. As the Scripture says, "He who receives his life by faith is made right by God."**

Notice that this verse says you are as righteous as God is. Now, you may be thinking, *No one can be as righteous as God is!* But the Bible doesn't say your *actions* are as good as God's actions. It says the Gospel is God's way of making you as righteous as Himself. It is a process you undergo as a believer that from beginning to end is fulfilled entirely by faith.

Receiving 'by Faith'

Now, what does that little term "by faith" really mean? For instance, when you ask someone, "Well, has your need been met?" he might answer, "*By faith!*" What is that person actually saying?

---

[2] C. S. Lovett, *Lovett's Lights on Romans* (Balwin Park, California: Personal Christianity, 1975), p. 31.

The person who has received the answer to his need *by faith* has gone first to the Word of God and found out that God has already given him the very thing he is about to ask for. That person then applies himself to what God has already said in His Word, receiving the answer to his prayer by faith. As he continues to believe God's Word, no matter what the outward circumstances say to the contrary, his answer manifests in this natural realm according to Matthew 21:22:

And whatever things you ask in prayer, believing, you will receive.

In Matthew 6:31 (*KJV*), Jesus presented a faith principle that can work for us either positively or negatively in the area of righteousness. He said we "take a thought" by *saying* it:

Therefore take no thought, saying, What shall we eat? or, What shall we drink? or, Wherewithal shall we be clothed?

How does that apply to receiving by faith the truth that you are righteous in Christ? Well, as you believe what God has said about you in His Word, you begin to talk to Him about it, telling yourself what you believe in the process: "Father, I just want to thank You that I am the righteousness of God in Christ. I believe Your Word that says the prayers of the righteous avail much; therefore, *my* prayers avail much, for You have made me righteous!"

But as soon as you pray that prayer, the devil starts talking to your mind: *You ugly thing, you.*

How dare you! You are so presumptuous to ever think God would do something for you! Look at how bad you are. It doesn't matter if you wait for the answer to your prayer for twenty years — you're still not going to receive it!

At that point, you have to decide which thoughts you're going to "take" or receive as true. Whatever thought you take determines the words you're going to speak. In fact, if you "take" the devil's thoughts of defeat and condemnation, after a while you'll forget what you prayed for in faith to begin with!

You see, God always does what He says He will do. But the day you don't think God will come through for you is the day the devil will talk you out of your miracle. The enemy will get you to thinking, *You know, I don't really deserve that anyway. God isn't going to do that for me.* If you keep thinking like that, one day you'll just say, *"Forget it — I give up!"*

All of a sudden, God has to stop working on your behalf. The angels who were bringing you the answer to your prayer are forced to put on the brakes and take a step back.

The Bible explains why this is so. Psalm 103:20 says, **"Bless the Lord, you His angels, who excel in strength, who do His word, HEEDING THE VOICE OF HIS WORD."** In Jeremiah 1:12 (*NAS*), God states, **"...I am watching over My Word to perform it."** Finally, Hebrews 1:3 says that God *upholds* all things by the Word of His power.

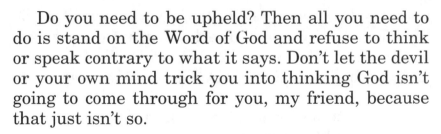

Do you need to be upheld? Then all you need to do is stand on the Word of God and refuse to think or speak contrary to what it says. Don't let the devil or your own mind trick you into thinking God isn't going to come through for you, my friend, because that just isn't so.

You know, there is really just one major thing in my life I've asked God for that still hasn't manifested in my life. I've already received all the other big things I've had to stand in faith for. In fact, I can't really think of anything else to request of the Lord because He's already blessing me more than I could have ever asked or imagined in every area of my life. He has more guts to give to me than I have guts to ask Him!

That's true for you as well. God is bolder in giving to you than you are in asking Him for something because His faith toward you is much greater than your faith toward Him. But I believe you and I are on our way to catching up with Him!

Now, let me say this to you as we long as we're talking about this subject of living by faith. Never allow this subject to become dull or boring to you. Don't ever think you know everything you need to know about faith. If that were true, why would you ever have even one unmet need? If you know all there is to know about living by faith, why would you ever have to deal with a bunch of wrong thoughts running through your mind?

There isn't one Christian who is such an expert at living by faith that he can claim to be walking in the complete freedom of all God has provided for him. That's why God **"...made Him who knew no sin to be sin for us..."** (2 Cor. 5:21). We *had* to be justified by faith (Rom. 5:1). The only way we could ever have peace with God was through our Lord Jesus Christ. Jesus died for the ungodly. He died for *us* so we could become righteous in Him.

Forsake Every Unrighteous Thought

In Isaiah 55, the prophet Isaiah shares something with us from the heart of God that can help us walk in the righteousness God has given us.

> **Seek the Lord while He may be found, call upon Him while He is near.**
> **Let the wicked forsake his way, and the unrighteous man his thoughts; let him return to the Lord, and He will have mercy on him; and to our God, for He will abundantly pardon.**
>
> **Isaiah 55:6,7**

Now, "the wicked" refers to the person who doesn't know God — someone who has yet to become a believer. On the other hand, the term "unrighteous man" refers to those who "live in neglect of plain duties" toward God.[3] This can refer to a believer who is out of fellowship with God.

What is this believer to do to get back in fellowship with God? He is to *forsake, turn away from,* and *push out of his mind* every unrighteous thought.

---

[3] Matthew Henry, *Matthew Henry's Commentary on the Whole Bible: New Modern Edition* (Electronic Database: Hendrickson Publishers, 1991).

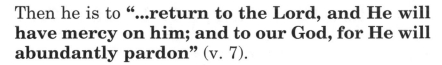

Then he is to **"...return to the Lord, and He will have mercy on him; and to our God, for He will abundantly pardon"** (v. 7).

In verse 8, the Lord goes on to say, **"For My thoughts are not your thoughts, nor are your ways My ways...."** Notice that God never said your ways or your thoughts are wrong; He just said His ways and His thoughts are *better*.

So often people think that God's thoughts and ways are not right. They think they know better than God, so they look for some way to work out their problems on their own. Then after coming up with their own solutions, they expect God to go along with them. They assume God is exactly the way they think He is.

Believe me, my friend, God is *not* the way you nor I nor any other natural man thinks He is. Stop anyone on the street, and ask that person, "What do you think about God? How do you think God treats people?" You'll find that people have all sorts of misconceptions about God. For instance, some say, "Well, I don't really think a loving God can send people to hell." That's one big misconception people have about God — that He is the one who comes down on people and sends them to hell.

But God isn't like that. He isn't like anything natural man can conceive. That's why He says in Isaiah 55:9:

> **"For as the heavens are higher than the earth, so are My ways higher than your ways, and My thoughts than your thoughts."**

Our thoughts are not God's thoughts. God's thoughts are so much higher than we can fathom. The way He thinks about us is so much better than the way we think about ourselves.

So in order to find out how we should think about ourselves, we have to go to the Word. The Word has the power to transform and renew our minds until we begin to think God's higher thoughts and live according to His higher ways.

That's what God is talking about in Isaiah 55:10,11:

"For as the rain comes down, and the snow from heaven, and do not return there, but water the earth, and make it bring forth and bud, that it may give seed to the sower and bread to the eater,

So shall My word be that goes forth from My mouth; it shall not return to Me void, but it shall accomplish what I please, and it shall prosper in the thing for which I sent it."

Notice that the rain and snow *make* the earth bring forth and bud. The earth has no choice — it *must* bring forth and bud when it receives its needed moisture.

Then God says, **"So shall My word be that goes forth from My mouth...."** This word "so" means *in the same way*. God is saying, "Think about the rain and snow that come down from the heavens, returning only after watering the earth and

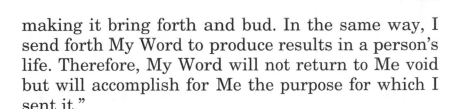

making it bring forth and bud. In the same way, I send forth My Word to produce results in a person's life. Therefore, My Word will not return to Me void but will accomplish for Me the purpose for which I sent it."

Thus, feeding on God's Word is the key to renewing the mind in the area of righteousness. Some Christians have a problem with this. They think that in order to have any good thoughts, they have to wrestle them out of God, as if God were trying to *keep* good things from them!

These Christians think, *As soon as I get my life straightened out, God is going to bless me.* But nothing could be further from the truth.

You know, there is no one more miserable in life than a Christian who doesn't understand righteousness and is walking out of fellowship with God. A Christian in that position is absolutely confused. He has no clue whatsoever about what is going on in his life. His mind is filled with thoughts of guilt and self-condemnation. Meanwhile, God is endeavoring to draw him back to Himself, loving him and blessing him as much as He can.

You see, once you've known God and tasted His Presence, you become absolutely miserable if you get out of fellowship with Him. In your own mind, it's worse than before you were born again.

Just think about it. Isn't it strange how unsaved people seem to be able to cope with the adversities of life better than many Christians? As soon as a small problem arises in a Christian's life, the first thing he or she often wants to know is "What's wrong with me?"

Most of the time lost people don't sit around and think, *What's wrong with me?* Instead, they think, *Well, that's all right. I'll get through it. It's going to work out.* Then they just keep right on going.

You'd be amazed if you sat down with some unsaved people and found out how much horrible destruction is going on in their lives. So many times, you'd never know it by looking at them. Sure, they might be going through a difficult time, but they don't stop functioning in life. They know they have to keep on going if they're going to make it. And even though they're probably bothered by all their problems, they don't go around talking about those problems to everyone.

On the other hand, as soon as something goes wrong in our lives as Christians, too often we "come apart at the seams." You see, we have been preconditioned to failure. We've been told our entire Christian lives why our faith *isn't* going to work. We've been told God is trying to teach us something through our adversities. We've been given a poverty brain. We've been given a sickness brain. We've been given a guilt complex brain that makes us feel like we're at fault, no matter what bad thing happens in our lives.

So we live our lives feeling guilty all the time. "There's something wrong with me. That's why God isn't blessing me — because there's something

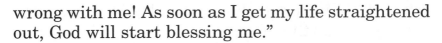

wrong with me! As soon as I get my life straightened out, God will start blessing me."

Once again, nothing could be further from the truth. Remember, our thoughts are not God's thoughts. The way God thinks about us is a great deal better than the way we think about ourselves.

God thinks about you wonderfully. He thinks you're really fun to spend time with. He likes to hang around with you. He already knew all about your little quirks and idiosyncrasies, and yet He still saved you.

In fact, your idiosyncrasies were worse the day you got born again than they are today. So why would Jesus want to hang around with you when you were first born again, only to decide later that He wants nothing more to do with you because you seem to be missing the mark? That doesn't make sense.

Of course, you may be allowing all kinds of thoughts that don't make sense to run through your mind, including the lie that you'll never be able to make the grade in your Christian walk. If that's true, you're probably constantly praying, *Oh, God what do You want me to do with my life? What do You want me to do?!?*

But the truth is, most of the time when you're asking God what He wants you to do with your life, you're already doing it. How do you think you got where you are today? God has placed you in the position you find yourself right now to bless you, leading you even when you didn't know it!

You may be waiting for God to tell you something else to do. But it's important to accept the fact that God is already working in your life both to will and to do according to His good pleasure, satisfaction, and delight (Phil. 2:13).

You have already "made the grade" in God's eyes. Through Jesus' redemptive work on the Cross, God sees you as *righteous* — just as if you had never sinned a day in your life. All you have to do now is get your thinking straight and start seeing yourself the same way!

4

GOD HAS ALREADY
QUALIFIED YOU!

Understanding righteousness is such an important part of learning how to think God's higher thoughts, or how to "acquire saved brains." The failure to understand righteousness is the number-one reason why Christians quit in the area of prayer. It is the number-one reason why Christians feel guilty. It is the number-one reason why Christians live "works-oriented."

People who don't see themselves as being the righteousness of God think, *Oh, if I could only be different. Maybe someday I will be righteous.* Righteousness is always something they're grasping for. But as we've seen, righteousness is something they have already *become* through the new birth! God has already qualified them to live an abundant life filled with His blessings!

Acting on the Engrafted Word

I want to explore the Word further on this subject of righteousness. We need to find out what God has to say about us so we begin thinking His higher thoughts.

The book of James has some things to say that can help us renew our thinking about how God sees us. First, James 1:21 (*KJV*) says this:

Wherefore lay apart all filthiness and superfluity of naughtiness, and receive with meekness the engrafted word, which is able to save your souls.

The Word of God is already engrafted down on the inside of you. Therefore, you don't need to get the Word of God *in* you. You need to get the Word of God *out of* you.

That applies to this subject of righteousness as well. You are already the righteousness of God whether you ever realize it or not. If you did everything in your life absolutely perfectly from this moment forward, you still wouldn't be any more righteous than you are right now. You see, righteousness isn't achieved by what you have done; righteousness is given because of what *Jesus* has done. It is Jesus' work of redemption that has qualified you as the righteousness of God in Him.

James 1:22 (*KJV*) goes on to tell us what happens if we neglect to apply the engrafted Word to our everyday lives:

But be ye doers of the word, and not hearers only, deceiving your own selves.

Perhaps things haven't been working out for you in life, and you can't figure out why. It is possible that you are deceiving yourself into thinking you're doing what the Word tells you to do.

"But aren't you talking to me about proving my faith by doing a bunch of works?" you may ask.

No, I'm talking to you about *the engrafted Word.* I'm saying that the Word of God isn't just something to gather dust on your bookshelf. God's Word isn't something you put on your coffee table so you can open it when the pastor comes over to visit and pretend you've been reading the Word. That isn't what you're supposed to do with your Bible — you are to live it, think it, speak it, *do* it!

How To Avoid Deceiving Yourself

When you hear the Word but don't apply your life to it, God says you are deceiving yourself. This word "deceive" can also be replaced with the word "delude," which essentially refers to *fooling yourself so completely that you believe a lie is the truth.* "Deceive" can also mean *to have subjective fantasies about yourself* and *to lead yourself astray.*

That term "lead astray" implies that you are being taken by the hand and led away from the path of truth. But how do you have subjective fantasies about yourself? Well, you might think, *Hey, I'm doing the Word. I'm believing it.* Meanwhile, the biggest part of what comes out of your mouth is focused on your problems rather than on the promises in God's Word. In that case, you're indulging in the subjective fantasy that you're a doer of the Word!

My friend, if you're doing the Word of God, why do you spend even one minute complaining about your problems? Why do you allow a carnal mindset that produces about three seconds of God's Word out of your mouth to every twenty minutes of the problem?

I find it amusing but sad when people tell me they're believing God for a particular need to be met and then spend the rest of the time complaining to me about that unmet need. These people have subjective fantasies about themselves and are therefore leading themselves astray.

Now, look at verse 23 (*KJV*):

For if any be a hearer of the word, and not a doer, he is like unto a man beholding his natural face in a glass.

The word "glass" here refers to a handheld mirror. After the man looks at himself in this handheld mirror, the Bible says he **"...goeth his way, and straightway forgetteth what manner of man he was"** (v. 24 *KJV*).

Now, what manner of man *was* he? This doesn't necessarily refer to something the man was doing; rather, it was how he saw himself in God's Word. He went his way, forgetting what God had revealed to him about who he was in Christ.

Here's the picture this scripture paints of you if you are a hearer and not a doer of the Word. You look into the Word of God and find out what it says about you. For instance, you may read Second Corinthians 5:21 and think to yourself, *Yes, that's the truth! God has made me righteous in Christ. That's wonderful! It's so exciting to see myself the way God sees me!*

But then as you go your way, you forget to take your "mirror" with you. In other words, you don't meditate on the Word, keeping it before your eyes and uppermost in your mind. Suddenly those same old negative thoughts start running through your mind: *I never do anything right. Every time I try to do something, I always end up a failure.* Without your "mirror," you soon forget what you look like in the Word as you let those carnal thoughts paint their own dark picture inside of you.

A lot of Christians make that mistake. They know how to talk the "God talk." When they're in church, they are like fire! But when they step back into the routine of daily life, they're not like fire any-more. As a matter of fact, they're not even a little spark! When pressures come, they give up on the Word of God and revert to the world's way of dealing with their problems.

Now, let's take a look at Verse 25 (*KJV*):

But whoso looketh into the perfect law of liberty, and continueth therein, he being not a forgetful hearer, but a doer of the work, this man shall be blessed in his deed.

The term "looketh into" means the man *peers* down and sees himself not just in a handheld mirror, but in an entire wall of mirrors — in other words, the "perfect law of liberty"!

This is not talking about the law of the Old Covenant. This man is looking into the perfect, complete, New Covenant law of freedom. And he doesn't start out one way and then end up another. He doesn't start out in that which God says about him and end up in religious legalism. No, he *continues* in the perfect law of liberty. No matter what he is doing, he is continually looking into the mirror of God's Word. He peers down into it and sees that he is the righteousness of God in Christ, and he steadfastly lives according to that revelation.

This man is **"...not a forgetful hearer, but a doer of the work...."** Notice that the phrase has changed. He is not only a doer of the *Word*; he is a doer of the *work*.

That doesn't mean you have to do good works in order to be right with God. It means that as you digest the Word of God, you begin to do the works of Jesus.

In John 6:28, Jesus was asked this question: **"...What shall we do, that we may work the works of God?"**

Jesus replied, **"...Believe in Him whom He sent"** (v. 29). Just believe on Jesus. That's all you need to do in order to work the works of God.

How can we perform miracles? How can we touch people's lives? How can we help people find their divine destiny? Through believing both in the living Word, Jesus Christ, and in the written Word of God.

As we meditate on the Word of God throughout the day, a picture of ourselves doing the Word will form on the inside of us. When it does, we will automatically begin to act on the Word of God in our lives. That's when we become "doers of the *work*." That's when we become abundantly blessed in all that we do!

So how does all this apply to you? My friend, until you are continually peering into the perfect law of liberty that says you are the righteousness of God in Christ, you may preach its truth to all your friends, but it still won't work for you.

Maybe you have just enough of the Word of God to get under your skin and *bother* you, but not enough to *bless* you. It actually irritates you to read God's promises because you're not seeing them come to pass in your life.

If that's the case, you need to look into the mirror of the Word and remind yourself every day of what God says about you. You need to admit, "If blessings are not coming to pass in my life — if I'm not free in my mind from pressures, problems, guilt, condemnation, and fear — it isn't someone else's problem; it's mine. I need to peer into the perfect law of liberty until God's truth pushes every trace of deception from my mind!"

Think about it. Why should you try to pay for something with guilt and condemnation that Jesus already paid for? That's called double jeopardy! There is no such thing as double jeopardy, neither in this nation's justice system nor in God's justice system. You can't pay for the same crime twice.

So don't be a person who just looks at the Word and then forgets what it says. Be like the man James talks about, who peers into the perfect law that gives every man freedom. Be a person who continues in the Word and never quits.

"Yeah, but it doesn't look like it's working in my life!"

No matter what it looks like, you must not quit.

"But how long is it going to take?"

I can't tell you that. Nevertheless, *you must not quit.*

You see, it isn't a question of how long it will take for God's Word to work in your life. In fact, the day you stop thinking about how long it's going to take is the day it will begin to work!

So don't quit too soon and settle for far less than God intended. Allow God's Word to be the number-one authority in your life for the rest of your life. In every situation, let this be your attitude: "I don't want to know what anyone else thinks. I'm just interested in knowing what *God* thinks about this subject."

You and I could try to figure out together why you're not experiencing victory in your life. We could even agree on the answer. But that won't do anything for you. If all you're looking for is an emotional back rub, forget it. You will only find your answer by acting on the engrafted Word that calls you righteous in Christ. In the mirror of God's Word is the freedom that causes you to be blessed in all you do!

Victory Is Up to No One Else But You

Too many Christians shy away from examining themselves according to the Word to find out why they're experiencing problems in their lives. It's easier to blame circumstances or other people for their failures. But blame-shifting actually comes from a lack of righteousness consciousness.

Do you realize it was a lack of righteousness consciousness that made Adam hide from God? God called out, "Adam, where are you?"

Adam replied, "I'm over here hiding."

God asked him, "Who told you that you were naked?"

Adam said, "Well, you know, that woman You gave me made a mess of things."

A person who is feeling condemnation from a lack of righteousness consciousness seldom wants to take responsibility. It's usually someone else's fault. And when you want to talk to that person about something he needs to change in his life, he often wants to turn the situation around and talk about what is wrong with *you*.

Thank God, that is one mistake I learned to avoid early on in my Christian walk. Soon after I began to believe the Word of God, a man ministered the Word of God to me for eight hours in one day. My life has never been the same.

This man didn't pull any punches. He let me know I had a long way to go in spiritual maturity and that it was up to me and no one else to get in the Word and start growing up.

But I didn't mind his straightforward manner. I had come to this man because he had something I wanted. I wanted what he knew about God.

To this day I've never seen a person walk in more righteousness than that man. He understood righteousness. He didn't care what other people thought. Only what God thought meant something to him.

That day I learned I was the righteousness of God in Christ. I learned I was completely separated from my past. I no longer cared what happened to me before that moment. It didn't matter to me anymore.

You may ask, "Yes, but don't you feel bad about what happened in your past?"

When you're the righteousness of God, you don't have to feel bad because you know God isn't imputing your sin to you. If He isn't laying any sin to your charge, why should you?

God doesn't want you wasting your time feeling guilt and condemnation. He wants you to believe what He says about you. You are righteous in Christ — now *think*, *speak*, and *act* like it's true!

A Change in Covenants

It was so important to God to make man righteous before Him that He even changed covenants with him. Hebrews 8:6-8 explains this change in covenants, speaking of Jesus and the ministry of the High Priest:

> **But now He has obtained a more excellent ministry, inasmuch as He is also Mediator** [the Arbitrator, the Agent, the Negotiator, or the Go-Between] **of a better covenant, which was established on better promises.**
>
> **For if that first covenant had been faultless** [free from imperfection], **then no place would have been sought for a second.**
>
> **Because finding fault with them, He says: "Behold, the days are coming, says the Lord, when I will make a new covenant with the house of Israel and with the house of Judah."**

Now, the first covenant included the command-ments of the Mosaic Law. The Law was necessary after the people of God decided they no longer wanted a relationship with Him. They told Moses, "We want you to be our go-between between us and God. We can't stand to hear His voice. It makes us fear and quake and tremble. So, Moses, we want you to hear God's voice for us" (Exod. 20:18,19).

Because the people "stood afar off" from the Presence of God's Spirit, God had to give them com-mandments to live by in order to prolong their exis-tence as a people. You see, in its degenerated state, humanity will continually spiral downward when not upheld by God's Presence.

In verse 7, God tells us what He thought of this first covenant: **"For if that first covenant had been faultless...."** God wouldn't have said that unless the first covenant had fault in it — and the truth was, it was *not* free from imperfections. Otherwise, there would have been no reason to seek another covenant if the first one worked.

Then in verse 8, God said, **"Because finding fault with them...."** Finding fault with whom? With His people. You see, God has always dealt with His people according to His covenant with them. So when He looked at man through the first covenant and saw fault in him, God said, "I must change the covenant I have with man. He will never be able to keep the commandments I have given him."

Why did God need to change the covenant? He changed it so He would no longer see fault in you.

If under the Old Covenant you could have gotten right with God by your own works, there would have been no need for a change in covenant, and Jesus wouldn't have had to shed His blood. Why? Because you would have been able to make it on your own.

So just get rid of this whole idea that you can do anything in life in your own strength. The way you received Jesus is the very same way you do everything in your Christian life. It doesn't work to sit back and think, *I need to figure out what to do in this situation.*

Personally, I don't want to figure out *anything* on my own! I know that even when I think I have something figured out, I don't! I start to do something that I think is going to fix the situation, but it only keeps me from hearing the right answer from the Lord.

Why do you think there are more than 1,100 Christian sects in the United States of America? Because so many of them are focused on telling you their particular way to fix your life on your own — by the way you dress, the way you talk, where you go or don't go, what you drink or don't drink, what words to use or not to use, etc.

You can't get right with God through your own works or mental reasonings, so don't waste your time trying. Just stay willing to continually change as God shows you new revelation from His written Word, and you will never become stagnant or self-deceived in your spiritual walk.

He Remembers Your Sin No More

Hebrews 8:10-13 goes on to tell us why this New Covenant is so much better than the former one:

"For this is the covenant that I will make with the house of Israel after those days, says the Lord: I WILL PUT MY LAWS IN THEIR MIND AND WRITE THEM ON THEIR HEARTS; and I will be their God, and they shall be My people.

"None of them shall teach his neighbor, and none his brother, saying, 'Know the Lord,' for all shall know Me, from the least of them to the greatest of them.

"For I will be merciful to their unrighteousness, and THEIR SINS AND THEIR LAWLESS DEEDS I WILL REMEMBER NO MORE."

In that He says, "A new covenant," He has made the first obsolete. Now what is becoming obsolete and growing old is ready to vanish away.

What a profound promise! God says that, under the New Covenant, He would implant His Word upon our innermost thoughts and write them in our hearts!

People often say, "You have to get the Word down in your spirit." But, actually, that isn't true. As I said earlier, you don't need to get the Word *in* your spirit; you need to get it *out*!

Your problem is not that you have no Word down on the inside of you; otherwise, you could take credit for all the wonderful things God has brought forth in your life. God has implanted His Word in your mind and written it on your heart, so you *can't* take credit for anything. Your challenge is to renew your mind through that Word. You must acquire "saved brains"; then you'll comprehend that the day you were born again was the day you died and cut that line between your past and present.

Once that line was cut in my own life, it wouldn't have mattered if you had screamed at that person I used to be or called him every name in the book. That guy has already died. He's dead, and it's not nice to talk against the dead!

Someone may try to remind me, "Yes, but look at what you did just yesterday, Robb." It's all under the blood of Jesus. In fact, God doesn't even know what that person is talking about!

Do you know that that's exactly the way God treats you as well? You may say, "God, look at all the times I've messed up lately!"

But God just replies, "What are you talking about?" Verse 8 tells us why — He remembers your sins and iniquities no more!

Somehow we have gotten the wrong idea about God. We think we have to wrestle blessings out of Him or twist His arm to get something out of Him. But God is doing all He can to get us to believe what He has said so He *can* bless us!

That's why Deuteronomy 28:2 says, **"...All these blessings shall come upon you and OVER-TAKE you...."** Blessings have to chase most Christians because they are usually running the other way, thinking, *Oh, no, not me! I don't deserve that!* Meanwhile, God has already promised to be merciful to their unrighteousness and to remember their sins and iniquities no more!

Why is it that we often fight for the right to remind God of what we do wrong? God already told us that He doesn't remember anything we have ever done wrong. *He* said that, not some preacher. Yet we sit around remembering all the horrible things we've done wrong while people are going to hell at the rate of 22,000 a second!

If God doesn't remember your sins anymore, you shouldn't even bring them up to Him. Psalm 103:12 says, **"As far as the east is from the west, so far has He removed our transgressions from us."**

So what is the truth about you? *That which is written.*

Believe in Jesus' Sacrifice

Some preachers just don't understand the magnitude of God's mercy and grace toward His people. These preachers unwittingly hold you in bondage by tying God's approval of you to legalistic laws and commandments. They teach that if you will perform certain things, God will give you a reward at the end of the day. Or they give you nineteen steps to follow to get right with God.

Well, before I knew any better, I did all nineteen steps, and those steps didn't help me at all! Why not? Because God had already done everything that was necessary to make me right with Him!

God made a new covenant with man through the blood of His Son, and now He sees no fault in humanity. More than anyone else in the entire universe, God believes in the sacrifice of Jesus. He has absolute faith in that sacrifice, even if you and I don't!

Most Christians believe in the sacrifice of Jesus intermittently. When they're doing well, they believe in Jesus' sacrifice. But when they're doing badly, they think they have lost it all. These people have it backwards. The time they really need to believe in the price Jesus paid for them is when their backs are against the wall and it looks like they are going down for the count. That's when they need Jesus more than ever!

You Can't Earn Your Own Righteousness

The book of Romans also has some important truths to teach us as we endeavor to renew our minds in this area of righteousness. In Romans 1, the apostle Paul talks about the heathen man, or the unsaved man who is without God. Then in Romans 2, Paul talks about the religious man.

When Paul gets to the third chapter, he says in essence, "It doesn't matter whether you're unsaved or religious; both of you are in the same spot. You're both under sin. Neither one of you are free.

Religious man, you may look like you're doing real well, but you are not. You have insulated yourself from the truth about God's Word with a bunch of religious junk."

In Romans 3:19 and 20, Paul is quite clear in stating his position:

> **Now we know that whatever the law says, it says to those who are under the law, that every mouth may be stopped, and all the world may become guilty before God.**
> **Therefore by the deeds of the law no flesh will be justified in His sight, for by the law is the knowledge of sin.**

What does verse 20 mean when it says, **"...by the law is the knowledge of sin"**? Well, just think about all those times you have tried to establish your own righteousness by setting up certain "commandments" in your life to follow. Every time you try to establish your own set of commandments, you end up violating them.

For instance, you might decide, *I'm going to get up at four o'clock every morning to pray.* The first morning you get up and pray at four o'clock. That night you set your clock again to get up at four o'clock. But when the alarm clock goes off the next morning, you roll over and go back to sleep.

So tell me something — do you now feel condemned because you didn't keep the commandment you set up for yourself? Yes, you do, because "by the law is the knowledge of sin."

Every time you try to earn your righteousness by following self-imposed laws, you'll end up disappointed with yourself. Let's go back to that example of prayer. Maybe you've decided it's time to develop some discipline in your prayer life. But instead of seeking God about the matter, you set up your own little plan for accomplishing your goal.

You meditate on the Word and confess daily, "When I pray, God gives me my answer in the Name of Jesus. The Father loves me, and He gives me good things when I ask Him. John 14:14 says that if I ask, proclaim, demand or say anything in Jesus' Name, He will do it. Matthew 21:22 says that whatsoever things I ask for in prayer believing, I shall receive it."

Finally, you say, "Okay, I'm ready to pray!" So you start praying, believing you receive your answer in the Name of Jesus. But as soon as you begin praying, suddenly you experience resistance. You never thought you wouldn't receive your answer before you prayed, but now all sorts of negative thoughts are running through your mind. You think, *This is a waste of time. I probably won't get it. Look at what's wrong with my life. Look at how badly I missed it yesterday. God isn't going to answer my prayer.*

Just like that, your self-made plan for a disciplined prayer life flies out the window!

So just accept it — you can't establish your own righteousness by trying to keep either Old Covenant laws or a bunch of manmade laws. That's why Paul said in Philippians 3:9 that your goal should **"...be found in Him, not having [your] own righteousness, which is from the law, but that which is through faith in Christ, the righteousness which is from God by faith."**

Your own righteousness, derived from trying to keep the Law, will get you nowhere. Jesus has already done everything that needs to be done for you to be righteous. Therefore, your righteousness comes from God by faith in Jesus.

It's that simple. You're not getting anything you deserve. If you did, you would be in trouble! I guarantee you, friend, you don't want what you deserve. You may have been praying, "God, I want my rights! I want justice!" But take my word for it — you *don't* want justice. You want the mercy, the grace, and the righteousness that Jesus has already bought for you with His blood!

Paul says something similar in Romans 3:21,22 (*KJV*):

> **But now the righteousness of God without the law is manifested, being witnessed by the law and the prophets;**
> **Even the righteousness of God which is by faith of Jesus Christ unto all and upon all them that believe: for there is no difference.**

The righteousness of God is apart from the Law — *not* because of it — and it is being manifested, or made continually plain, by God. Also, notice that this right-eousness is **"...by faith of Jesus Christ...."** (v. 22 *KJV*). You see, when you obtain anything from God, you obtain it by the faith of Jesus Christ. You are actually plugging into what Jesus has already received for you.

Some Christians walk around wearing their answers to prayer like badges. "Oh, yeah," they brag, "I believed for this, and I got it!" They try to outdo one another with the answers to prayer they can manifest with their "faith."

What a joke! Honestly, all those people did was believe what Jesus had already done for them. They didn't produce the answer. God produced it, and they were the beneficiary of it.

That's why God is so preeminent in everything. We can't accomplish one thing without Him — and that certainly includes establishing our own right-eousness! Remember, Jesus said, **"...For without Me you can do nothing"** (John 15:5). Jesus did it all. We are righteous only because of Him.

The devil may talk to your mind, saying, *You are something else! Look at how bad you are. Look at those negative things you did.* But all you have to do is tell him, "You're right, devil. However, there are two facts you're not taking into account. Number one, I didn't become righteous on my own. Number two, thank God for the faith of Jesus Christ!"

Paul goes on to say in Romans 3:23,24 (*KJV*):

For all have sinned, and come short of the glory of God;
Being justified freely by his grace through the redemption that is in Christ Jesus.

Why is it that we are all familiar with what verse 23 says — that we've all fallen short of God's glory — but not what verse 24 says? Because we've been conditioned all our lives to believe what is *wrong* about us.

But the truth is, we have been justified freely by God's grace because of Jesus:

Whom God hath set forth to be a propitiation through faith in his blood, to declare his righteousness for the remission of sins that are past, through the forbearance of God.

Romans 3:25 *KJV*

Jesus Christ was the divine Gift of love for the salvation of man, given so man could become righteous in God's sight.

Believing God's Word
Produces Righteous Actions

You can't establish your own righteousness, but Paul tells you who can:

...In His forbearance God had passed over the sins that were previously committed,

to demonstrate at the present time His righteousness, that He might be just and the justifier of the one who has faith in Jesus.

Romans 3:25,26

The word "just" in verse 26 comes from the same word translated "righteous." So in effect, Paul is saying, "...that God might be righteous and the righteousness of him who has faith in Jesus."

God is your righteousness because you believe in Jesus. Your righteousness doesn't come from what you do. You are not the one who brings good things to pass in your life.

Verse 28 presents the final conclusion:

Therefore we conclude that a man is justified by faith apart from the deeds of the law.

There is absolutely *nothing* you can do in order to be righteous before God. But understand this: If you really believe that God is your righteousness and that therefore *you* are righteous, your faith will produce actions. You won't be able to stop your righteousness from manifesting as righteous deeds in your life.

Why, then, do so many Christians talk one way and behave another? Well, remember, no one has a gift to live this Christian life. What Paul said in Philippians 2:12 is absolutely the truth — believers have to work out their own salvation with fear and trembling!

That means you have to believe the Word and build it down on the inside of you until it causes those righteous actions to manifest. It doesn't work to rely on someone always saying to you, "You need to stop doing that and start doing this. Do this. Stop doing that. Don't do this." At best, trying to live righteously that way only works for a short amount of time.

For instance, I have absolutely no desire to smoke a joint of marijuana. I also have no desire for someone else's wife. None. Zero. That doesn't mean I don't think women are pretty. I actually think God never made an ugly one! The reason I don't desire another woman is that I'm in love with God; I'm in love with my fellow man; and, finally, I'm in love with my wife.

Some people may say, "The only reason you don't commit adultery is that you love your wife."

No, I know a lot of men who love their wives, yet still commit adultery. Why do they do that? Because they don't love their brother. You see, love works no ill to his neighbor (Rom. 13:10). Therefore, if these men believed God's Word, they wouldn't work ill toward their neighbor. Instead, they would remain faithful to their wives because *believing God's Word produces righteous actions*.

Walking by the Spirit
Or in the Flesh?

If we don't earn our righteousness through the Law, does that mean the Law has no validity? Paul essentially asks that question in Romans 3:31 (*KJV*): **"Do we then make void the law through faith?..."**

Paul answered that question by saying, "No way! We *establish* the law."

Many Christians have actually taught that the Law doesn't matter. They claim that the Law has passed away.

But the Law has *not* passed away. The Law is actually in great standing. However, that doesn't mean you are supposed to work on *keeping* it. In fact, you can always tell whether you are walking by the Spirit or walking in the flesh by this one thing: Are your thoughts always pushing you to keep the Old Covenant commandments?

For instance, you may deal with these kinds of thoughts all the time: *Is this the right thing or the wrong thing to do? Well, let's see, the Bible says, "Thou shalt not lie," so I guess I better tell the truth.*

Now contrast that with the thoughts of someone who is walking by the Spirit and not by his senses: *I'm a new creature, and lying has to do with the old creature. Old things have passed away, and all things are new. Therefore, I speak the truth in love!*

Always remember — your flesh is ugly, and it will use the Word of God against you. In fact, the flesh gets its power from do's and don'ts. It will even use the Ten Commandments to make you feel guilty.

Paul says that rather than nullifying the law through faith, we actually establish it. In other words, we look at the Law and say, "The Word of God is true; therefore, the Law is true, holy, and just. Nevertheless, I thank You, Jesus, for making me righteous by Your blood, because in my own strength, I cannot keep the Law!" That's when you know you're walking by the Spirit and not by your senses.

I know a lot of people who pride themselves in having their lives all together. Everything is organized; rules have been set up for every situation. They are ready to handle any problem that may arise in their lives. But the truth is, they are living by their own set of laws rather than by the Spirit. What will they do when a problem comes along that is bigger than they are? These people have one recourse, just as everyone else does: They must look to the Word of God for their answer.

Sin Is Not Laid to Your Charge

God is your righteousness; therefore, you have the ability to stand in God's Presence as if sin had never existed, free from accusation and the sense of guilt, inferiority, or failure. You cannot be accused of wrongdoing because it would be double jeopardy. Jesus already paid the price. You have already been qualified to live in rightstanding with God.

This is the cornerstone of your Christianity. This is the cornerstone of your ability to get your prayers answered. This is the cornerstone of your ability to believe God for anything that is part of your spiritual inheritance.

Do you realize that you can't even believe for your healing unless you believe you're righteous? Why is that? Because as soon as you get sick, the devil condemns you and tells you *why* you're sick! *You sucker!* the enemy whispers to your mind. *This sickness is a result of all the times you messed up!* The devil also likes to use well-meaning people to make you feel unworthy through their flowery "words from the Lord."

When someone comes to me and says, "The Lord has given me a word for you," I think, *First, let me strap on my helmet, face mask, chest protector, shin guards, knee pads and bulletproof vest!* Then after inwardly preparing myself, I say, "Yes, Brother, what is it?"

"The Lord will heal you as soon as you get the sin out of your life."

Oh, boy, I think. *I'm glad I put on my armor first!*

How many people have been told over the years that the Lord would fill them with the Holy Ghost as soon as they took off their jewelry or started dressing right? In other words, the message they are given is that God will do something for them spiritually as soon as they do something physically.

But that just isn't true! Galatians 2:16,17 tells us why:

"Knowing that a man is not justified by the works of the law but by faith in Jesus Christ, even we have believed in Christ Jesus, that we might be justified by faith in Christ and not by the works of the law; for by the works of the law no flesh shall be justified.

"But if, while we seek to be justified by Christ, we ourselves also are found sinners, is Christ therefore a minister of sin? Certainly not!"

You are not justified by works. And if you don't receive your salvation by works, you can't *lose* it by works!

What if you seek to be justified by Christ and you are found to be a sinner? Is Christ therefore the minister of sin? No, He is not. He didn't bring that sin into your life. But He is also not judging you by it!

David understood this truth even in his day. He said in Psalm 32:1, **"Blessed is he whose transgression is forgiven, whose sin is covered."**

What an incredible revelation that God showed David! *Blessed is the person whose sin will not be laid to his charge.* This is the central truth that needs to be uppermost in our thoughts as we renew our minds with the Word!

My friend, sin has not been laid to your charge. There is nothing in your past, present, or future that

Jesus is holding against you. That is precisely what it means to be righteous!

When some people hear that, they get angry and think, *That's blasphemy!* But just search the Scriptures, and you'll find out what I'm saying is true. For instance, look at Romans 4:25-5:1:

> **Who [Jesus] was delivered up because of our offenses, and was raised because of our justification.**
> **Therefore, having been justified by faith, we have peace with God through our Lord Jesus Christ.**

Jesus was delivered up on account of our trespasses. He wasn't put to death because of what *He* did wrong. He was delivered over to Satan and his hordes because of what *we* did wrong — past, present, and future!

You may protest, "But if that's true, I could go out and do anything wrong I wanted to, and God would still love me!"

Let me ask you this: Now that you've learned God is not laying sin to your charge, does that make you want to go out and do something wrong? If you love the Lord, I doubt if you are now thinking, *Boy, oh, boy, it's okay to sin! I can't wait to hit the party scene with everything I've got!*

So don't let it bother you when I say there is nothing you can do that can separate you from the love of Christ. Understanding that truth won't lead you into sin — it will set you free!

Facing Adversity Unintimidated

It is imperative that you believe you are who God says you are. You will find that understanding your righteousness makes a big difference when you face situations in which you would normally feel intimidated.

You see, intimidation results from a lack of righteousness consciousness. Of course, there is a difference between being cocky and sarcastic and knowing you're the righteousness of God. Some people will tell you that you are very presumptuous to go around saying God is going to move on your behalf. But the reason you can say God will come through for you is that you're convinced of His faithfulness and your righteousness in Him. You're not proud. You're not presumptuous. You just know what God has said.

I'll give you an illustration of this. I worked for a well-known parcel delivery service a number of years ago as a parcel driver. I tell people that I went to Bible college on a delivery truck and conducted my field ministry outside the truck — casting out devils, healing the sick, and leading people to Jesus when I went up to their door. It was a wonderful experience during which I learned a lot.

I remember a particular incident during one Christmas season that taught me how to stand on my righteousness in Christ. At the time, I was delivering about 525 parcels per day. Each delivery included getting out of my truck, walking to the back of the truck, retrieving the right package,

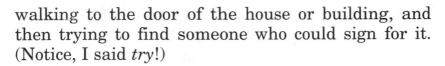

walking to the door of the house or building, and then trying to find someone who could sign for it. (Notice, I said *try!*)

Now, remember, this was some time ago. I realize this company has changed the way it does things now. But at the time, it was a kind of unwritten law among parcel drivers that, in case no one was around, a driver needed to make sure he got rid of his packages one way or another. That didn't mean he would throw the package in the river; it just meant he was to find a place to put it where the recipient could find it.

That Christmas season I had a new route in a suburb outside Chicago. The first time I went there, my superior just handed me a map and a truck filled with packages and sent me on my way.

Once I reached the town, I stopped and pulled out my map. This was the only town I had ever seen in my life whose streets looked more crooked than a pile of spaghetti noodles! At night, the town had no street lights — just little gas lights about every 500 feet.

Now, a little gas light provides a great atmosphere if you want a candlelight dinner. But gas lights don't help much when the houses are 100 to 150 feet off the street and you can't see the house numbers! Consequently, I was driving all over the place, having a terrible time locating my delivery destinations.

Every Christmas season, I had to deliver a lot of fur coats. One day I delivered a fur coat to the home of a new person in town. No one was home, so I left it where it would most likely be found by the homeowner. However, the woman later called and said she never received it.

I went back to the home and talked to the woman. I said to her, "Ma'am, there must be some kind of mistake. I delivered the package. Didn't you receive it?"

She smiled and said, "No, I never received it."

So I went back to my superior and told him what the woman had said. He said, "Well, we'll see what we can do."

The next day my manager came back to me and said, "Robb, it was your responsibility, so you'll have to pay for this fur coat."

Now, you need to understand that, at this particular time in my life, a fur coat was "megabucks." And I had already made the decision that the devil wasn't going to steal anything from me. In fact, I had determined to make that character pay for anything he ever took from me.

So when my manager said, "You're buying the fur coat," I said, "No, I don't think so."

Look, Robb," he said, "this isn't a joke. I'm telling you, you have to buy this fur coat."

I replied, "Sir, with all due respect, I don't really care who pays for it, but I'm not."

As I walked out of the office, I thought, *Thank God, I am the righteousness of God in Christ Jesus. God is going to take care of this situation!*

The next evening when I returned from making my deliveries, two Loss Prevention detectives were waiting for me. They came out to me with a pay voucher that would authorize deducting a certain amount from my paycheck every week in order to pay for the fur coat.

The two men put the voucher in front of me and said, "Sign right here."

I said, "I don't think so. No, I'm not going to sign."

My boss came out and said, "Robb, would you please sign this paper?"

I said, "No, the devil isn't going to steal from me. It doesn't matter to me who pays for the jacket, but I'm not paying for it."

My boss said, "They say that *you're* paying for it. Do you understand that?"

I replied, "No, Sir, I don't. God bless you, but I don't understand those words right now."

One of the Loss Prevention men said, "Look, he doesn't go out in the morning unless he signs this paper."

My boss pulled me aside and said, "Will you *please* sign this thing?"

I said, "No, Sir, I won't. If it means my job, that's okay. Meanwhile, I need to go home and talk to my Counselor."

When I arrived home that night, I immediately went before the throne of God with the Word in hand. I prayed, "Lord, Your Word says that if any man sin, he has an Advocate with the Father. Jesus, I'm asking You to be my Advocate in this situation. I know I may have made a mistake in leaving that fur coat where I left it. But I also know this — He who knew no sin was made to be sin for me so I could be made the righteousness of God in Him! It doesn't matter what I did. It doesn't matter what went wrong. What matters is what Jesus did for me!"

So I went in the next morning, got in my truck, and left to make deliveries. I was always the fastest of the parcel drivers, so when I returned, the building was empty. I went in, completed all my paperwork, punched out on the time clock, and went home.

The next day I came in and did the same thing. Every day I kept coming to work, and every day the devil told my mind, *This is it. You're losing your job today. This is it — you're fired!*

But every time I'd talk right back to the devil and say, "No, I don't accept that! He who knew no sin was made to be sin for me so I could be made the righteousness of God in Him. I'm holy, unblamcable, unaccusable, and unreproveable, without fault or failure in my Father's sight. I am what the Word of God says I am!"

So three weeks went by without a word from my boss about the matter. As you might imagine, the wait was like a boil under pressure. Every day when I'd go in to work, that pressure would come on me, and I'd start confessing, "No, in the Name of Jesus, I won't lose my job! He who knew no sin was made to be sin for me!"

I'd go home at night and pace the floor, speaking the Word over the situation: "He who knew no sin was made to be sin for me. Jesus paid for any mistake I made concerning that coat. Even if what I did was wrong, Jesus paid for it. And if Jesus paid for it, then, praise God, there's no such thing as double jeopardy! If He paid for it, it's already been paid for, and I'm not paying for it."

Finally, after three weeks of this kind of pressure, I went to my boss and said, "Hey, I need to ask you something. Whatever happened about that fur coat?"

"Oh, forget it," he said. "We took care of it another way."

All I could say was *"Praise God!"*

You might say, "Well, you were wrong to leave that fur coat the way you did."

Yes, you're right. I was wrong. I never said I did it right. All I said was that because I am the righteousness of God, I knew God would take care of the situation — not based on what I did, but based on what *Jesus* did.

The same thing is true for you, my friend, no matter what situation you're facing in life. You need to come to the place where you recognize within yourself that you are separated from your actions. You are separated from your past. You are separated from everything that's going on in this world.

Until you come to that place in your life, the devil can deceive you into being what he wants you to be every day. He can put you in a corner. He can drag you back into the natural and keep you from living in the supernatural. He can pull you into the trap of looking at yourself according to your actions instead of according to God's Word. And as long as you let the devil do that to you, you can never be happy.

You will only be happy when you learn to view yourself as God views you. Why do you think you have mood swings? Why are you up one day and down the next? Because you're looking at yourself through your own carnal eyes.

The reason I don't change in my moods is this: I don't view myself with me in mind; I view myself with *Jesus* in mind. Hebrews 13:8 says Jesus is the same yesterday, today, and forever. Well, if He's the same yesterday, today, and forever, then so am I, bless God!

You see, the glorious thing about the Gospel is that Jesus has given us beauty for ashes, the oil of joy for mourning, and the garment of praise for the spirit of heaviness (Isa. 61:3). That term "garment of praise for the spirit of heaviness" is translated this way in the *Moffatt's* translation: God has given us **"...a corneal for a cornak...."** In other words, He has given us a *crown* or a *diadem* for a *song of death.*[4]

Jesus has given you a crown and raised you up far above what you could ever think or do on your own. He has made you as righteous as Himself, not based on what you did, but based on what He has done. That's why Jesus is Lord over all!

Fellowship vs. Relationship

Here's an important question for you: If our righteousness is based on what Jesus has already done, why do we have a need for First John 1:9?

If we confess our sins, He is faithful and just to forgive us our sins and to cleanse us from all unrighteousness.

This verse gives instruction on how to come back into *fellowship* with God, but it is not talking about your *relationship* with Him. You see, your relationship with God is not dependent on you; it's dependent on God.

Your parents determined whether or not you came into the world. Once you were born, you couldn't change your relationship with them as their child. However, your *fellowship* with your parents is dependent on you, not them.

---

[4] James Moffatt, *A New Translation of the Bible* (New York and London: Harper and Brothers Publishers, 1935), p. 814.

In the same way, your fellowship with God is dependent on you. If you choose to sin, your wrong action adversely affects your fellowship with God.

Let's talk a moment about what sin is. It is walking away from that which is written. It is stepping aside from the truth. It is not believing the Word of God. You see, your actions are based on what you believe. Therefore, sin results from believing incorrectly. Wrong actions come from wrong believing.

First John 1:9 provides the answer to broken fellowship through sin. You are to confess what you did that was outside the truth you are supposed to believe. In doing so, you are agreeing with God. That agreement gets you back on track again in your fellowship with Him.

What if you died after you did something wrong and before you got back on track again? Would you go to Heaven? Yes, you would. Why? Because your relationship is not based on you; it is based on God.

How Far Does Righteousness Go?

If righteousness could come any other way except by grace, then Jesus died for nothing. But how far does righteousness go? It goes as far as you are free from religion. When religious thinking holds you in bondage, righteousness can rise only to the level of your failure and your unbelief. In other words, as soon as you mess up, you no longer believe you are righteous before God.

But if you stop believing you are the righteousness of God when you do something wrong, what good is that righteousness? You must not need it because you are obviously depending on your own performance for God's approval!

The truth is, you *do* need the righteousness God has given you through Christ. That's why God wants you to be completely divorced from your past and from natural thoughts. He wants you to renew your mind with Second Corinthians 5:21 so you can experience your righteousness as a daily reality, even when you stumble and sin.

In order to acquire "saved brains," you have to get rid of the mindset that says God blesses you because you are good. God blesses you because you believe, not because you are good. He doesn't have favorites.

You may say, "Well, Robb, God just comes through for you because you're a preacher."

But I wasn't always a preacher, and God was just as faithful to answer my prayers then as He is now.

Of course, that doesn't mean I'm anywhere close to perfect. Believe me, there are things about me as a person I do not like. But because the love of God has been shed abroad in my heart by the Holy Spirit who has been given to me, I love myself. I believe what God says about me more than I believe what I sometimes feel about myself.

It should be the same way with you. My opinions shouldn't matter to you. You should want to know what *God's Word* says about any given subject. Therefore, when I speak God's Word, both of us should hit our knees, submitting ourselves together to the Word of God.

You have been made the righteousness of God. What does that mean to you? You cannot be intimidated or controlled if you truly believe that. How can you stay trapped underneath someone's thumb when you've been made the righteousness of God through the mighty redemptive work of Jesus Christ?

Just believe what God said about you. Never allow yourself to be affected by what others say about you. They can say whatever they want to say — you have determined that you will believe what *God* said. If you'll do that, you'll be happy. If you don't, you'll constantly be tied to what you see in your natural mirror every day.

Jesus is my Champion. I'm free because of what He has done for me, not because of what I have accomplished. I believe what God says in His Word about me; therefore, it's very easy for me to separate myself from my identity as Robb Thompson so I can be completely identified with Jesus Christ.

How do you become grounded in a solid understanding of your righteousness in Christ? Well, number one, you sometimes have to pursue that understanding with gritted teeth. You see, it isn't always easy to believe you're the righteousness of God while you're still dealing with your flesh.

Number two, you must meditate on the Word concerning this subject. Spend time in the Word of

God, and allow the Word to do your fighting for you. Remember Exodus 14:13 and 14, where Moses told the Israelites, "Stand still, and see the salvation of your God. The Lord will fight for you as you just stand firm and believe."

That's what you have to do. Even when you feel like you're nothing but a failure, even when your mind goes to great lengths to tell you otherwise — stand firm on the foundation of what *God* says about you. Believe that you are already qualified — the righteousness of God in Christ according to the Word!

5

LET GO OF THE PAST

O ne of the most important steps to take as we renovate our minds is to *let go of our past*. Many of us have a very difficult time doing that. We may claim that we have done it, but our thoughts, words, and actions often say otherwise. And because we continue to live in our past, we miss out on receiving God's best for our present and our future. That's why it's vital that each and every one of us let go of our past once and for all.

You might think, *I've forgotten my past so many times, I can't count them!* But if you had truly forgotten the past, all you'd see when you looked in the mirror would be a smiling face. You'd be able to look at yourself and say with confidence, "You know something? You are the righteousness of God. There is no fault or defect in you. You are the greatest. God loves you so much."

The truth is, most people don't do that. Instead, they look in the mirror and start rehearsing all the things that are wrong about themselves. They talk about all the times they missed it and how many times they've failed. They moan about how things aren't really working out for them in life. They meditate on all the negative things that have happened to them over the years. They complain that they are the living fruit of the bad things other people have done to them in the past.

Your Outcome Is Determined By Your Response

But you can't blame others for the way your life is right now. It's true that you weren't able to determine where you came from. You couldn't plan your parentage or your genes. You couldn't choose the kind of household you would grow up in. You couldn't determine the way people treated you as a child.

However, the outcome of your life is not determined by what other people do to you or say about you. The outcome of your life is determined by how you *respond* to what other people do and say about you.

As you read this, you may be thinking, *Yes, but I am like this because of what So-and-so did to me when I was a young child.* Or maybe you're thinking, *The reason I've never had the kind of breaks I've needed in life was that other people always got in my way.*

You can either choose to forgive and let go of all those hurts, or you can choose to hold on to them. It is your decision, but understand this: *Your mind can never be renewed by the Word of God until you first allow that Word to change you.*

I know a particular husband-and-wife ministry team who never felt like they got their deserved break. According to this couple's perspective, the devil had selected them as special targets to harass and to hinder. Not only did they think the devil was after them, but they thought other Christians were against them as well, stopping the flow of God's blessings in their lives.

But that isn't the way it works. What the devil or another person says about you or does to you should never change what you believe about yourself. Your source of knowledge is God's Word — *not* the devil, nor other people. Therefore, every situation you confront in life can make you *bitter*, or it can make you *better*. You are the one who determines the outcome.

Never let yourself fall in the trap of believing what other people say about you. Don't even focus on the *good* things they say about you. Jesus said, "Beware when all men speak well of you" (Luke 6:26). Why did He say that? Because when all people speak well of you and you start believing your own press releases, you become susceptible to creating subjective fantasies about yourself. You begin living in a fantasy world. You see, you're really not as good as other people think you are. But you're not as bad as *you* think you are either!

The only thing I am interested in is what God says about me. I appreciate it when people love me. I think it's really wonderful. I'm just like everyone else — I like to be loved, needed, and wanted. However, the outcome of my life is not determined by what any other person says or does. It is only determined by my choice to believe God's Word, no matter what.

Today Is the Sum Of Yesterday's Choices

Once we understand that the outcome of our lives is up to us, it becomes clear that *our future success depends on our willingness to forget the things that are behind us* (Phil. 3:13). Here's where we run into the problem I mentioned earlier. People often refuse to live for the future because they're still living in their past. In that case, their past actually ends up determining their future!

You see, the circumstances of your present life are a direct result of your past. The choices you made last year, the things you did, the level of effort you put into studying the Word of God — all these decisions have helped create the present circumstances you are living in right now.

Therefore, we must cut off two elements from our lives. Number one, we must cut off our past. Number two, we must cut off present thoughts and actions that do not proceed from our new life in Christ.

Your future is largely determined by the thoughts you allow yourself to dwell on today. So don't get upset if you run into problems in the future because of the wrong thinking you have allowed your mind to dwell on today. If you let your mind think on any negative thought it wants to, you have no right to get upset when you reap the consequences later on down the road. You allowed those consequences to happen!

As I've gone through life, I have noticed there are really only three types of people: 1) people who only live in their future (these are the people who are always telling you what they are going to do "someday"); 2) people who continually dwell on their past (these people often blame their present performance and circumstances on what someone did to them in their past); and 3) the precious few who know how to live completely in their present to create a God-directed future.

If you fit in one of the first two categories, there is a way you can change the course you're taking right now. You don't have to go in the direction you're going. You don't have to receive the thoughts you've been receiving. You can live your future differently than you've lived your past!

But to do that, you must get this truth deep down on the inside of you: When you were born again, you were completely separated from your past. Every negative thought you ever harbored, every fault that worked against you since your youth, every bad habit or stronghold that bound you and caused you to struggle, every destructive comment people attempted to lay on you, *everything* that contradicts the person you have become in Christ Jesus — *all* of that is dead. None of it sticks to a person who, according to First Corinthians 6:17, is one with the Lord: **"But he who is joined to the Lord is one spirit with Him."**

Therefore, none of it is true any longer about *you*.

A Balanced View of Yourself

Some Christians make the mistake of thinking they have "arrived" in their spiritual walk. Assuming they have reached a place of spiritual maturity other believers only dream of, these people tend to think they are right on every issue. On the other hand, many other Christians are constantly plagued by thoughts of failure and defeat. These believers just can't seem to let go of the hurts and disappointments of the past.

More than likely, you also know in your heart that you've made some mistakes and wrong decisions since you became a believer. But that doesn't mean those mistakes have to affect your present walk with God. Think about it — why should past failures cause you to stumble today? What good does it do to hold on to your hurt and your pain? It does absolutely no good at all.

In fact, you do nothing but hurt yourself when you go through each day thinking you're wrong about everything. And you hurt yourself just as much if you walk around thinking you're *right* about everything! There has to be a balance in your life regarding how you relate to both your past failures and your past successes.

'I Thought I Could Do No Wrong'

When a person doesn't have this scriptural balance operating in his life, he is on dangerous ground. For instance, the Church suffered a great setback several years ago when a prominent minister fell into sin. Later when the minister tried to explain why it happened, one statement he made was very significant. He said, *"I thought I could do no wrong."*

That's what happens when God's Word ceases to be the central focus of a person's life. He can become so enamored with himself that he begins to think he can do no wrong. He might not articulate it to himself, but he develops the attitude that he knows more than God does. He begins to think his personal thoughts and experiences go beyond that which is written.

At that point, it becomes easy to make emotional decisions that are very wrong. For instance, he may think, *Well, I know God's hand has been on my life. He has blessed me up to this point. So I think I'll go ahead and act on what I've been thinking about. Everything will turn out fine because God is a forgiving God and He's on my side!*

That's what happened to that prominent minister who fell into sin so publicly years ago. This man was one of the greatest evangelists in modern-day history. More people are going to be in Heaven because of that man than anyone can even imagine. But this minister had a problem — he allowed himself to dwell on wrong thoughts about women. And because he had developed the attitude that he could do no wrong, Satan was able to use his uncontrolled thought life to bring him down.

I get concerned when I talk to ministers who are tremendously gifted, but whose character in contrast seems very small. They remind me of Proverbs 24:10, which warns, **"If you faint in the day of adversity, your strength is small."** The bottom line is this: Whenever *any* believer begins to think his own opinions and thoughts go beyond that which is written, he is headed for a hard fall.

What we allow ourselves to think is such an important key to putting our past behind us. Another crucial key is knowing how to scripturally deal with past sin so we can put it behind us.

Christians often miss it in this area of dealing with sin. After making the bad decision to act contrary to the Word, most believers go to God and cry out, "Lord, forgive me!"

But remember, we don't need to ask God to forgive us because we are already forgiven. God can't give any more forgiveness than He has already given us. If we had to constantly ask for forgiveness, the power in the blood of Jesus wouldn't be all-encompassing.

All God ever told us to do was to confess our sin, and He would forgive. As we cite the sin we committed, we are condemning that sin in agreement with

God because He has already passed a sentence on it. The matter is already taken care of as far as God is concerned.

So if forgiveness is not even a issue when dealing with your past sin, what *is* the issue? Well, let's think back to the case of that prominent evangelist. I remember seeing him repent on television. Tears were flowing freely down his face as he confessed his sin before the television audience and before God. It was wonderful that he was willing to do that. However, the main thing that needed to happen in his life may never have happened. *He needed to deal with his mind.*

Remember, he got in that terrible situation because he believed he could do no wrong. So if he never dealt with his wrong thinking — if he never renovated his mind — he is still in danger of making more bad decisions!

Today this evangelist can still preach the Gospel and see thousands upon thousands of people get born again. Why? Because Romans 11:29 (*KJV*) says, **"...The gifts and calling of God are without repentance."** That divine call on his life didn't leave just because he messed up. Nevertheless, the knowledge that his character doesn't match his gift will eat him alive if he doesn't learn to control his mind with God's Word.

You and I are no different. We are the ones who decide whether the Word of God or the word of the devil will control our minds. Whichever voice we listen to in our thought life is the voice that will win out.

The High Price
Of Paul's Wrong Choice

I recently had a conversation with a minister who said something along this line. He told me, "You know, Robb, everything I ever touched in the ministry turned to gold — until one day when I started thinking I could do no wrong. That's when I missed it *big!*"

As I listened to this minister, it reminded me of what happened to the apostle Paul. In Acts 20:23, Paul told the elders of the Ephesian church that the Holy Spirit had been witnessing to him in every city that bad things would happen if he went to Jerusalem. Everywhere he went, believers were telling him, "Paul, don't go to Jerusalem. Don't go there, Paul. Don't do it!"

God was attempting to get a message to Paul, but Paul didn't want to hear it. You see, when Paul was a young man, he had been a member of the Jewish Sanhedrin, an important person among his people. Paul had always had great affection toward the Jews. Unfortunately, he allowed that affection to override what God wanted to do in his life.

The desire of Paul's heart was to see the Jews come to the Lord. He also wanted to prove his ministry to the Gentiles to the elders of the Jerusalem church, many of whom were very skeptical. Thus, one of the reasons Paul wanted to go to Jerusalem was to give the needy Jewish believers a monetary gift from the Gentile churches in a gesture of brotherly love.

So in Acts 20:22-24, Paul gives his response to all the warnings he had received about going to Jerusalem:

"And see, now I go bound in the spirit to Jerusalem, not knowing the things that will happen to me there,

"except that the Holy Spirit testifies in every city, saying that chains and tribulations await me.

"But none of these things move me; nor do I count my life dear to myself, so that I may finish my race with joy, and the ministry which I received from the Lord Jesus, to testify to the gospel of the grace of God."

Paul said that the Holy Spirit was already telling him that bonds and afflictions awaited him. But then he said, "None of these things move me. What the Holy Spirit is telling me about Jerusalem doesn't move me. What people are telling me that God is showing them doesn't move me."

Why didn't these things move Paul? Because he made the wrong choice of thinking he could do nothing wrong!

Then Paul said, "I don't count my life as being dear to myself. But I want to finish my course with joy. I want to fulfill the ministry I have received of the Lord Jesus to testify of the Gospel of God's grace. I'm going to go do that in Jerusalem. I'm also going to take on those Jerusalem elders who don't understand my ministry to the Gentiles!"

Later in Acts 21:8 and 9, Paul visited the home of Philip the evangelist in Caesarea. While there, Paul heard from Philip's four daughters. The Bible says they all prophesied to Paul. More than likely they told him by the Spirit the same thing he had been hearing from many other believers — that he was not to go to Jerusalem. The message was clear: "Paul, don't go. Paul, don't go. *Paul, don't go.*"

But just as Paul hadn't listened to the many believers who had warned him before, he also didn't listen to the four women who prophesied to him. Finally, God sent Agabus the prophet — "Mr. Big Stuff." Agabus was the most well-known prophet in the entire Church of that day. When he spoke forth the word of the Lord, the walls shook!

Agabus walked into the room and immediately took Paul's belt, using it to bind his own hands and feet. Then he prophesied:

"...Thus says the Holy Spirit, 'So shall the Jews at Jerusalem bind the man who owns this belt, and deliver him into the hands of the Gentiles.'"

Acts 21:11

Once more God was telling Paul, "Paul, don't go. Paul, don't go. No, no, no, no! *Don't go.*"

But Paul said, "Why do you want to break my heart by saying these things? Why do you want me to stop? I'm going to do what I believe God wants me to do." Yet the entire time, God was telling him,

"Listen, Paul. I'm trying to get through to you. Don't go!"

You see, Paul was determined to share the Gospel with the Jews who were enemies of the Cross of Christ. But there was a problem with Paul's desire. God was warning him not to go. Paul went anyway, though, because he wouldn't let go of where he had come from. He wouldn't let go of his past.

When Paul arrived in Jerusalem, he had an interesting meeting with James and the other elders of the church. James told Paul, "My brother, look at the myriad of Jews who believe. If they find out you are here, they are going to be ticked off. So this is what you need to do: go purify yourself according to Jewish law. Take with you these four men who have taken a vow, and pay for their purification. If you will show that you keep the Law, God will bless you for it." (*See* Acts 21:20-24.)

And guess what? Paul said, "Okay"! He broke every principle he had been teaching about the grace of God! He went back under the Law, thinking it was the right thing to do.

But it wasn't the right thing to do. While Paul was inside the temple completing the ritual of purification, a riot broke out about him. The Jews falsely accused him of taking some of the Gentiles into the temple, which caused a huge uproar inside the temple (vv. 27-30).

From that moment on, Paul was never free for the rest of his life. As a result of his wrong choice to go to Jerusalem, he was taken out of active ministry and spent four years in prison. That wasn't God's will, so why did it happen? Because Paul had begun to think that he was above the witness of God's Word and that he could do no wrong. He didn't need anyone else's counsel. He didn't need anyone ministering to him.

As a result of this wrong perception, Paul attempted to take authority over something God clearly did not make him responsible for — ministry to the Jews. In Galatians 2:6-9, Paul said himself that he wasn't called to minister to the Jews:

> **But from those who seemed to be something — whatever they were, it makes no difference to me; God shows personal favoritism to no man — for those who seemed to be something added nothing to me.**
>
> **But on the contrary, when they saw that the gospel for the uncircumcised had been committed to me, as the gospel for the circumcised was to Peter**
>
> **(for He who worked effectively in Peter for the apostleship to the circumcised also worked effectively in me toward the Gentiles),**
>
> **and when James, Cephas, and John, who seemed to be pillars, perceived the grace that had been given to me, they gave me and Barnabas the right hand of fellowship, that we should go to the Gentiles and they to the circumcised.**

When Paul arrived in Rome as a Roman prisoner, he continued to try to reach out to the Jews. He called the Jewish believers together to stand up for what he believed, but he didn't receive the response he was looking for. The Jews of Rome didn't even know what he was talking about!

And it came to pass after three days that Paul called the leaders of the Jews together. So when they had come together, he said to them: "Men and brethren, though I have done nothing against our people or the customs of our fathers, yet I was delivered as a prisoner from Jerusalem into the hands of the Romans...."

Then they said to him, "We neither received letters from Judea concerning you, nor have any of the brethren who came reported or spoken any evil of you...."

And some were persuaded by the things which were spoken, and some disbelieved.

So when they did not agree among themselves, they departed after Paul had said one word: "The Holy Spirit spoke rightly through Isaiah the prophet to our fathers,

"saying, 'Go to this people and say: "Hearing you will hear, and shall not understand; and seeing you will see, and not perceive...."'

"Therefore let it be known to you that the salvation of God has been sent to the Gentiles, and they will hear it!"

And when he had said these words, the Jews departed and had a great dispute among themselves.

Acts 28:17,21,24-26,28,29

Some people say, "Well, it was God's will for Paul to be in jail so he could write the epistles." Does that mean he couldn't have written them in Antioch or Corinth? Couldn't he have written them while sitting on the beach somewhere? Why did he have to be in prison in order to write the epistles? That doesn't make sense to me.

"Well, God put Paul in jail because He was trying to work something good in his life."

I don't know how Christians can justify God doing wrong. God didn't put Paul in jail. If Paul had listened to God in the first place, he never would have attempted to go to Jerusalem! No, Paul lost his freedom when he made the wrong choice in thinking he could do no wrong. As a result of holding on to his past, he overstepped his spiritual authority and forfeited his spiritual balance.

Letting Go of Wrong Associations

In order for you to get where God wants you to go, you must make sure you don't make that same mistake. For instance, you may be trying to hold on to who you were, what you used to do, or whom you used to hang out with in the past. That's dangerous. You're a new creation in Christ with a heart to obey God's Word. That means you need to make sure the people closest to you are those who hear the Word of God and do it.

I agree with Jesus' statement when He said, "My mother and my brothers are those who hear the Word of God and do it" (Matt. 12:50). Now, you may say, "Oh, that's just absolutely heartless." No, it's a scriptural principle designed to save your life!

Everywhere you turn, there is failure and disappointment. Everywhere you turn, people aren't doing what God wants them to do with their lives. The more you hang around with people like that, the more you begin to lose your motivation to get where God wants *you* to go.

Personally, I've decided that the sky is the limit for me! I have only one focus in life — to do what God wants me to do, and God pity the one who stands in my way! I have a task to accomplish, and I'm not relaxing until it's finished! I want to get on with the program. I want to do what God has called me to do. If that were not possible, I might as well die and go to Heaven!

If you can't fulfill the divine purpose you were born to fulfill, what are you here for? Why do you even want to grow older? So you can one day be disappointed that your body doesn't function the way it used to? So you can be placed in a rest home and watch your loved ones neglect you?

Or let me ask you this: Why do you want to make more money? So you can pay more taxes? If you can't make anyone happy with the money you already have, how do you think you're going to make people happy with more money? You're forgetting the real reason you're on this earth.

That's the way many of us are. We think, *I don't want to deal with heavy questions like "Why did God put me on this earth?" or "What is His plan for my life?" I want life to be fun!* So we busy ourselves with accumulating things and scurrying to all sorts of social activities. We are busy, busy, busy, *busy*.

"Hey, listen, Pastor," you might say. "I'm sorry I didn't come to church. I was just too busy."

That isn't an excuse — it's an admission of guilt. When you give an excuse for not fulfilling your responsibility, you are telling people that you're completely wrong and you know it. You're just doing "the crab walk" out of the situation, trying to back out of what you know you should be doing.

It's time to get back to pursuing God's purpose for your life. The past is gone, and tomorrow is going to come whether you like it or not. Tomorrow is just another opportunity for you to either beat up on the devil or for him to beat up on you. You are either going to win, or you're going to lose.

But it's the choices you make today that will determine which one it's going to be — and one of the most important choices you must make is *with whom you will associate*. You have to choose to let go of both *past* and *present* wrong associations if you want to win in your *future*!

I follow that principle in my own life. In fact, if my own mother didn't want to obey the Word of God, she wouldn't be in my closest counsel.

Now, you may say, "What about *my* mother? She isn't saved, so she certainly doesn't want to obey the Word of God." That doesn't mean you don't need to visit her, minister to her, and love her. I'm just saying you can't afford to keep close counsel with people who don't want to do God's will.

I'm telling you — whom you associate with will determine how far you go in this life. Just look around and evaluate the people you're hanging around with. Are they going somewhere? Do you want to go where they're going?

That's like asking the man over in the park if he wants to know Jesus. He says, "No, I want to go to hell."

You ask him, "Why do you want to go to hell?"

He replies, "All my friends are there! Ha, ha, ha!" No, that man really doesn't want to go to hell. He just says he does because he doesn't want to deal with the reality of his situation.

You need to deal with the reality of your own situation by asking yourself, "Do I want to go where my friends are going? Do I want to experience what my friends are experiencing?" If the answer is no, you need to get out of the same pot they're in!

Let me give you an example of what I mean. A Christian man who sincerely wants to walk with God went to the local bar with a couple of Christian friends. While there, this person ran into a girl he used to know. He thought, *She's really nice. I think I'll go talk to her.*

So he had a couple of drinks with her and then asked, "Hey, do you mind if I take you home?" The next thing he knew, he ended up in bed with her, and the next morning he felt horrible.

Then this man called me. (It's funny how people call me *after* they feel horrible rather than *before* they feel horrible! I haven't figured that out yet.) He told me he didn't want to do what he did. He knew before he did it that he shouldn't do it. But he ended up yielding to temptation anyway.

I didn't talk to this man about going to bed with the woman. Do you know what I talked to him about? The fact that he went to the bar in the first place!

"You would have never seen her if you had stayed away from that place," I told him. "You never would have been tempted to sleep with her. If you had stayed away from the place of temptation, you wouldn't have had a problem with temptation."

Someone else comes to me and says, "Well, I started taking drugs again."

I don't talk to this person about taking the drugs. Instead, I ask him, "Where did you get the drugs? Where were you when you got them?"

You see, those two things called "feet" that you have on the bottom of your legs can take you one of two places: They can take you where you want to go, or they can take you where you *don't* want to go.

You'll never find anyone who gets in trouble by going where his heart wants to go. People only get in trouble when they go where their heart *doesn't* want to go. And why do they go there? Because they won't give up their past.

These people say, "I don't want to be a part of that anymore." Yet they continue to associate with the wrong people and let themselves think about what they used to do before they were saved. Finally, their thoughts become action, and they let their feet take them where they don't want to go.

Regarding my own personal relationships, I look at it like this: If my friends decide they don't want to obey the Word of God, they are not my friends. Proverbs 13:20 says, **"He who walks with wise men will be wise, but the companion of fools will be destroyed."** Therefore, when a person walks away from the Word, I will not walk with him any longer. I can't afford to do it; I have a divine call to fulfill.

Do I still like people? Yes, I do. But the main thing I have in common with them is not that we both like cars, nice restaurants, or downhill skiing. There are a lot of people who like cars or downhill skiing, but that doesn't mean they are necessarily my friends. My friendships are determined by whether or not those people *do the Word of God*.

I had to deal with this question in regard to a friend of mine who was living contrary to the Word in one particular area. It was very difficult for me when I first realized that this was the case. You see, I love this friend, and he walks according to the Word in many other areas. Nevertheless, in this one area he was not in agreement with God's Word.

"But aren't you still friends?" Not in that area, we aren't. And there is no denying that my friendship with that person is not as solid as it once was.

"But shouldn't a close friendship supersede everything else in life?"

No, your friendships should be determined by who does the Word of God, not by who has similar personalities or belongs to the same boat club as you do. Then if your friend deliberately walks away from the Word of God, you are released from your relationship to that person because the friendship was based on God's Word — *not* on the fact that you're good buddies.

When God's Word is your "litmus test" to determine who your friends are, you can develop the most unlikely friendships. Your friend's personality and background may be very different than yours; yet still you may find that you are both alike in many ways. What is it that makes you alike? The Word of God. It's God's Word in your life that determines the outcome of your friendships, and it is the quality of your friendships that determines the outcome of your life.

Forgetting What Is Behind

Let's go back to the apostle Paul for a moment. While Paul sat in that Roman prison, he penned a letter to the Philippian church. In that letter, he spelled out what he had learned through his experience at Jerusalem:

Brethren, I do not count myself to have apprehended; but one thing I do, forgetting those things which are behind and reaching forward to those things which are ahead,

I press toward the goal for the prize of the upward call of God in Christ Jesus.

Therefore let us, as many as are mature, have this mind; and if in anything you think otherwise, God will reveal even this to you.

Nevertheless, to the degree that we have already attained, let us walk by the same rule, let us be of the same mind.

Philippians 3:13-16

First, Paul said, **"Brethren, I do not count myself to have apprehended..."** (Phil. 3:13). Paul was actually implying that at one time, he thought he had "arrived" and that he could do no wrong. He thought he knew the answers and that he didn't need to check in with God anymore.

But Paul learned that he could do nothing without Jesus. So while sitting in that prison, he wrote, "There is only one thing that is important enough to me to hold on to. I am going to forget the things that are behind me and press forward to experience the fullness of God's call on my life."

Now, that should be the most important thing to each and every one of us as well. We are to focus on who we are today in Christ and refuse to let yesterday hang on to us, dragging us down. That doesn't mean we are supposed to consider ourselves as those who have already "arrived" spiritually. But this one thing we are to do: we are to forget what lies behind us. In other words, we are to *assign our pasts to oblivion.*

Personally, I don't really care about what happened in my past. I know the devil will come and talk to my mind, saying, *Think about how bad you used to be! What about all those terrible things you once liked to do?* I also know how irritating those thoughts can be.

But we may as well get ready for those kinds of demonic attacks. I mean, the devil isn't going let us think God's Word all day without some form of opposition! The enemy is *not* going to say, "Listen, since you're a Christian, I think I'll just leave you alone. Go ahead — think about God's Word. Confess the Word. And the next time you go to pray for someone, go ahead and raise the dead. It's okay; I'm not going to resist you anymore because you're such a great guy!"

Not once in my life has the devil acted like he was ready to roll over and play dead for me. Anything I ever received from God, I had to fight for. The devil has made it very clear that he doesn't like me at all. For instance, recently our house was struck by lightning twice!

"But why didn't God protect you?" He did. Even though the lightning knocked the nails out of the ceiling and put a hole in my roof, our house didn't catch on fire. So I think God did all right!

Another lightning bolt went right in our swimming pool. That was a sight to behold! "But doesn't that bother you?" No, if there was any algae in that pool before, it's dead now!

"Do you think God is trying to show you something?" No! "Do you think the devil is trying to show you something?" Yes — that he doesn't like me!

But I don't let things like that bother me. I'm not looking for a demon behind every bush just because my house was struck by lightning. Besides, Linda and I had owned the same television for seventeen years, and after the lightning incident, the devil had to buy me a new one! I had been thinking about buying a new television for a few months, but I just hadn't had the time. When the lightning strike blew out our old television set, the insurance company paid for a new one.

One way or another, I know the devil has to pay me back when he tries to steal from me. That's why his attempts to disrupt my life don't bother me.

The devil wants to steal from you too. But rest assured — what the devil means for bad, God will always turn around for good. So don't let the devil's strategies bother you. Look at life with a smile on your face that comes from the joy in your heart. Forget the things that are behind, and push on toward the goal line!

Finally, Paul instructed us:

Therefore let us, as many as are mature, have this mind; and if in anything you think otherwise, God will reveal even this to you.

Philippians 3:15

Paul was saying, "Those of us who are mature should have this mindset: We are pressing forward to take hold, forgetting the things that are behind, and pressing toward the mark for the prize." *That's* how we are to think. Paul learned his lesson; now we need to learn ours!

Don't Be 'Stony Ground'

The parable of the sower in Mark 4 provides an important principle regarding forgetting the past. Look at what Mark 4:14-17 (*KJV*) says:

The sower soweth the word.
And these are they by the way side, where the word is sown; but when they have heard, Satan cometh immediately, and taketh away the word that was sown in their hearts.
And these are they likewise which are sown on stony ground; who, when they

have heard the word, immediately receive it with gladness;

And have no root in themselves, and so endure but for a time: afterward, when affliction or persecution ariseth for the word's sake, immediately they are offended.

Jesus uses the term "stony ground" to symbolize a hardened heart. Therefore, the seed sown on stony ground refers to people who receive the Word with gladness but have no root in themselves to allow that seed to grow into a great harvest. Why don't they have any roots? Their hearts are hardened; therefore, the Word of God can't grow deep into their lives.

These people are hardened to the possibility of allowing God to work completely in their lives. They live a life of no commitment; thus, they only endure for a time. When affliction or persecution arises for the Word's sake — in other words, when someone challenges the Word in their lives — they immediately get offended. In other words, they get mad as soon as someone comes against the Word and quickly give up on trying to obey it.

Get Ready for Opportunities To Take Offense!

How does someone come against the Word in your life? Well, suppose you decide you're going to walk in love according to First Corinthians 13 from this day forward. You're going to love every person who comes across your path. People are just the greatest thing since sliced bread!

You're having the most wonderful time in the world loving people. Then all of a sudden, someone starts acting in a less than loving manner toward you. You know you should be thinking, *Well, it doesn't really matter how he treats me. I'm going to love him no matter what.* But instead, you say, "Well, if that's the way he's going to treat me, I'm going to treat him the same way!"

Smarten up, believer. You'll never make it that way in your Christian walk. If you're going to believe the Word of God, you may as well get ready for people to take you to task. You may as well get ready for people to offend you and to take advantage of you. And if you decide to give up on the Word and hold on to the offense, you'll be the one who loses.

The devil will whisper to your mind, *Oh, look at how they treated you. That is so horrible and cruel! Not only that, but it isn't right! If they really loved you, they would never treat you that way. Loving people don't treat other people like that!*

I've never seen anyone with more opportunity to be offended than Christians. Let me tell you why. You may remember how it was when you used to go down to the bar. It was easy to find friendly people. Someone would say, "Hey, let's have another round while you sit down and tell me your problems. Yeah, it's going like that for me, too, but we're going to make it. What are you doing tomorrow? I'll meet you back here."

That's why Christians often say, "I used to have more fun with the people at the bar. Christians don't treat me as well as the people at the bar did." Or they'll say, "I didn't have this much trouble in my life when I was out in the world." People make those types of comments to me all the time.

Out in the world, the devil can do whatever he wants to with you. However, when you get born again, suddenly you have something in your life the devil wants, and he'll use every means within his power to defeat you.

Fortunately, it doesn't take a lot to beat the devil. The main thing you need to know about overcoming the devil is this: Don't get offended. Don't get mad. Just say, "No, I choose to believe God's Word and walk in love instead!"

Your Point of Offense Is Your Point of Failure

This problem of offense is one of the biggest problems you will ever have to deal with in your mind. You see, your point of offense is your point of failure. Let me say it another way: *Your point of success is determined by your point of offense.*

You may ask, "What do you mean by the 'point of offense'?" It is the point at which you refuse to believe what God's Word says about you. It is the point at which you hold on to something other than God's Word on the inside of you. It is at this point of offense that you start down the road to failure in your spiritual walk.

Why do many people get offended? Often the reason is that they haven't let go of their past. They think you are going to treat them the same negative way other people have treated them in years gone by. They don't believe you're going to treat them differently. Because they are trapped in their past, they live in a constant state of mistrust, thinking, *You're just like all the rest. You'll treat me the same way the others did.*

This situation is very common in marriages. It is also true in people's relationships with others.

Each and every one of us come into relationships with a certain amount of "baggage" — perceptions and emotions accumulated over the years from past offenses. Too often we judge other people by that baggage.

We see certain characteristics in those whom we relate to in various arenas of life, and we think, *I thought so. You're just like all the others.* We tend to be irritable and impatient with them because of the problems we're having inside our own minds.

But you should never make a person in your present pay for something that someone did to you in your past. Every person is an individual. Every situation is an individual situation. If you are thinking that way about someone in your life right now, you need to realize that you never got free from the person who offended you at some point in days gone by. It isn't the person in your present life who bothers you; it is that person in your past!

So why are you making the people in your life today pay for what happened yesterday? Because you never got rid of the past. *You are your own problem because you have been holding on to offense.*

We don't need to allow offenses to rule our lives. The Word of God has given each and every one of us true freedom, releasing us from our past at the moment of our salvation. But too often we hold on to the hurts of our past because we think freedom will hurt more than this bondage we're already in.

That is the lie the devil wants you to believe. But freedom never hurts more than bondage. The day you finally release the offenses and hurts of your past is the day you will begin to find success in life.

However, you can't stop there. After letting go of all past offenses, you also have to determine that you will never again take what other people say or do personally. You see, every time you do that, the Word of God is stolen from you. Any ground you may have gained, you risk losing in one moment of time. You still know what the Word says, but you can't enjoy the freedom of it.

That's why you must let the hurts go, both past *and* present. Just put them in God's capable hands, and once and for all, *let them go*.

Make It Easy for Others To Love You

You may not realize it, but your personality is adversely affected when you hold on to hurts and offenses. Hidden resentment and anger can manifest in negative ways that ultimately leave scars on your relationships with other people. You could very well be irritating the people around you and not even be aware that you're doing it!

Wouldn't it be nice if we made it easy for others to love us? When we make it difficult, we force people to slide over into what I call "impersonal love." They can no longer love you because of your wonderful qualities or the great things you do. Instead, they can only love you based on that which is written in the Word.

It would be wonderful if we walked in such a high level of unconditional love and forgiveness toward other people that everyone we met in life was able to love us with personal love. That's the kind of love that says, "I love you because of who you are. You're a great person, and you're walking on the Word of God."

God wants you to have friends. God wants you to be loved. And God wants you to be able to love other people. But the longer you force people to relate to you out of impersonal love, the longer it's going to be before you develop any close friendships. That's why it's so important that you *let go of past offenses*. As you do, your friendships with other Christians will be transformed.

And for every new offense that may occur, determine to deal with it according to God's Word. Tell your friend, "Listen, let's find out what the Word says about this situation. Let's do it God's way." Learn to love enough to let the other person make mistakes. Don't leave the Word behind just because you want to hold on to an offense.

This principle works especially well within your marriage. Perhaps you feel hurt because of things your spouse has done in the past. But you are wrong if you are placing the responsibility of your marital relationship on your spouse as a person. You need to place that responsibility where it belongs — on God's Word, not on your mate.

Personally, I have placed the responsibility of my relationship with Linda squarely on the Word of God, not on the way Linda reacts to me or feels about me on any given day. My love for her isn't merely based on the fact that I think she's sweet. My love for her is based on that which is written. Therefore, if I am ever tempted to feel offended or hurt by something she says or does, I just take the situation to the Word and determine to let it go before it ever takes root on the inside of me.

Let God Set You Free
From the Past

I encourage you to do the same. Let go of every offense that has ever held you back from God's best in your life. Replace all those hurt or angry thoughts with the truth of God's Word.

It won't do you any good to hold on to the past. Sure, you could keep trying to prove that you were right. But how far is that going to take you? You may have justified yourself in your own mind, but how does God see the situation?

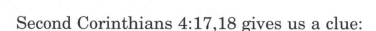

Second Corinthians 4:17,18 gives us a clue:

For our light affliction, which is but for a moment, is working for us a far more exceeding and eternal weight of glory,

while we do not look at the things which are seen, but at the things which are not seen....

According to this scripture, you have to stop looking at those "things which are seen" through the eyes of your hurt or through the eyes of the people who picked on you and never gave you the break you deserved. Instead, you must begin to look at every situation through the eyes of God's Word. After all, you are a believer. That means you believe in Jesus' power to set you free from your past!

I remember the day I set my faith on that truth. I hadn't been out of the mental institution very long when I read Second Corinthians 5:17:

Therefore, if anyone is in Christ, he is a new creation; old things have passed away; behold, all things have become new.

Now, I could have sat there and thought, *Boy, I sure hope that someday old things pass away! I sure hope that someday all things become new for me. Oh, God, please do something for me. Please let old things pass away. Please let all things become new.*

But I didn't do that. I just looked at that scripture and said, "'If anyone is in Christ...' Well, if I don't know anything else, I know I'm a believer. This says that if I am a believer, old things have passed away. And if something has passed away, it's dead.

"So everything that had to do with the guy who used to live inside this body before October 28, 1975, is dead — all the wrong desires; all the perversion; all the drugs; all the booze. Everything that was a part of my life before I came to know Jesus is *dead!*"

Now it's your turn to decide how you will respond to that scripture. What means more to you — who you are now, or who you were then? Who rules and reigns in your life — the new creature you have become in Christ, or the old you that God counts as dead?

You see, your old life can only live if you resurrect it from the dead. The devil cannot resurrect your past. He can scream all day long, but that doesn't change the fact that God says your past is dead.

However, *you* can resurrect your own past. You can say, "No, I'm not going to forgive. I'm not going to let go of the hurt." You can do that if you want to. But why would you want to?

Why would you want to let your bitterness and hurt make you rotten inside with sickness? Why would you want to live your entire life holding on to past hurts and offenses until you end up as a shriveled-up, bitter old person?

Why would you let the devil to win, not only in the life of the person who offended you, but also in your own life and in the lives of the generations who will come after you — just because you refused to obey the Word of God? Why would you want to do that when you can be completely liberated from your past right now by obeying the Word?

Ephesians 4:32 tells you exactly what to do to be free:

And be kind to one another, tenderhearted, forgiving one another, even as God in Christ forgave you.

The truth is, forgiveness isn't as big of a deal as you think it is. Forgiveness is merely releasing someone from something he or she has done.

Don't wait until you get to Heaven to find out how easy it actually is to forgive and let go of your past. Get real with yourself. Admit that the problem has been you and not someone else. Be honest enough with yourself that you can say, "Hey, I want freedom, so I am never going to allow myself to be offended again. I give up all the hurts and offenses. I give up all the pain. I let it all go."

Then make the quality decision that you won't give in to the hurt anymore. Start believing that someone loves you for a change. Believe that someone thinks you're good. Believe that people want to give something to you instead of always expecting them to take something away.

Don't make everyone else in the world pay for your hurts. Give them up to the Lord once and for all. Tell Him, "God, I just want to be completely free in my mind and in my life. I'm not willing to put up

with the hurts and offenses of my past any longer."
Then accept your deliverance from the past in Jesus'
Name — once and for all!

6

THE LIFE-OR-DEATH POWER OF WORDS

One thing you inevitably learn on the path to renovating your mind is the life-or-death power of *words*. Number one, you find out that *thoughts are only words that have yet to be expressed*. Number two, you discover that *words are containers of power*.

The truth is, you can kill a person a lot faster with your words than you can with a gun. A few cruel words of harsh judgment can actually cut a person so deeply that no human could ever heal him, adversely affecting the way he sees himself for the rest of his life.

The Negative Side of Words

I want to ask you a few questions so you can consider them as you read this chapter:

- Have words ever been spoken to you that you have found difficult to deal with?

- Have those words continued to stick with you throughout your life?

- Were words spoken to you while you were growing up that have caused you to react to others in a particular way?

I remember some things that happened to me as I was growing up that came extremely close to destroying me forever. If God hadn't intervened, I *would* have been destroyed. First, God sent one of His laborers across my path to help me receive Jesus as my Savior. Then He taught me how to get into the Word of God. Without the Word in my life, I wouldn't have made it.

I know the power in words. Remember, I was born again in a mental institution. I know what it means to be crazy and how a person can degenerate to that condition, largely through the power of negative words.

Here's how it can happen: Negative words are spoken to a child, both to his face and behind his back. He hears other people of consequence in his life — a teacher, a parent, a coach, his peers — degrade him, make fun of him, and call him names.

The child hears negative words so much that he begins to believe that those words define who he is. He turns inward as the words eat away at him on the inside. Satan then systematically and by design brings people into his life that will cause those words to come to pass in his life. Little by little, he begins to *become* those words, and the only thing that can ever set him free is the living Word, Jesus Christ.

The book of Proverbs has quite a bit to say about the negative side of words. Let's look at just a few of them.

1. In Proverbs 6:2, it says, **"You are snared by the words of your mouth...."** In other words, you are *taken captive* and *placed in prison* by the words of your mouth!

2. Proverbs 10:19 says, **"In the multitude of words sin is not lacking, but he who restrains his lips is wise."**

3. Then in one version of Proverbs 12:18, it says this: **"A man's careless talk stabs like a sword, but what a wise man says heals."**

4. Proverbs 14:15 states another principle about words: **"The simple believes every word, but the prudent considers well his steps."** My friend, don't believe every word you hear — especially when it is contrary to God's Word!

5. Proverbs 15:1 tells us that **"a soft answer turns away wrath, but a harsh word stirs up anger."**

6. Finally, Proverbs 15:4 says, **"A wholesome tongue is a tree of life, but perverseness**

in it breaks the spirit." Now, the word "perverseness" refers to a breach in the spirit caused by persisting in stubbornness and in deviating from the truth. A perverse person will persistently get into error and fault all the time. Therefore, you could read verse 4 this way: "A wholesome tongue is a tree of life, but persisting in stubbornness will cause you to walk in error or fault."

The Positive Side of Words

We can see some of the benefits of life-giving words in the scriptures mentioned above. Now let's look at a few more scriptures about the positive side of words.

1. In Romans 10:8, it says that **"...the word is near you, in your mouth and in your heart (that is, the word of faith which we preach)."** The Word is close to you. It is in your mouth and in your heart so you can *do* it.

   You see, whatever you have in your mouth and in your heart, you can do. That doesn't mean you *might* be able to do it; it means you *can* do it. The Word you meditate on in your heart and speak with your mouth becomes the Word you live day by day. Therefore, as you continually put the Word of God in your mouth, you find out you *can* do all things through Christ who strengthens you (Phil. 4:13)!

2. The book of Proverbs tells us some of the benefits of positive words. Proverbs 12:25 says this: **"Anxiety in the heart of man causes depression, but a good word makes it glad."**

3. Proverbs 15:23 says something similar: **"A man has joy by the answer of his mouth, and a word spoken in due season, how good it is!"**

4. Proverbs 25:11 says the same thing another way: **"A word fitly spoken is like apples of gold in settings of silver."**

5. Isaiah 50:4 says, **"The Lord God has given Me the tongue of the learned, that I should know how to speak a word in season to him who is weary. He awakens Me morning by morning, He awakens My ear to hear as the learned."** God wants to use you to speak a word in season to those people who are weary. He wants you to speak *good* words.

6. Finally, Ephesians 4:29 says, **"Let no corrupt word proceed out of your mouth, but what is good for necessary edification, that it may impart grace to the hearers."** The word "corrupt" here refers to something that is rank, foul, or putrid.[5] We are to avoid at all costs thinking and speaking words that are rank, foul, or putrid. Our words should be

---

[5] Fritz Reinecker and Cleon L. Rogers, *A Linguistic Key to the Greek New Testament* (Grand Rapids, Michigan: Zondervan Corp., 1976, 1980), p. 534.

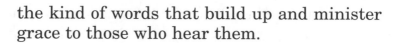
the kind of words that build up and minister grace to those who hear them.

Speaking Life Over Your Children

When you realize how powerful words are, you begin to understand why it is so important for you as a parent to love your children with words. You should continually speak good things over your children.

Just as Jacob laid hands on his children and blessed them at the end of his life, you can do the same. Lay your hands on your children and bless them in the Name of Jesus. Speak the Word over them, believing that the good things you speak *will* come to pass.

I speak wisdom over my son Anthony all the time. I believe he has the wisdom to lead God's people. He has the wisdom to win in life.

"What do you want your son to do for a career?"

I don't really care as long as he has the wisdom to lead God's people. If he has God's wisdom in his life, he's going to end up doing what God wants him to do. I don't determine what God wants him to do; *God* determines that. My job as his father is to do what I can to get him ready for it.

But what happens when parents speak negatively over their children? Their words become the starting point of their child's failure in life. That's just how dangerous it is to speak wrong things over one's children.

Let's talk about homosexuality as an example. Suppose a young boy is ridiculed and often called a "queer" as he is growing up. Suppose also that his father rejects him and tells him that he is less than everyone else. The father never hugs his son or gives him the kind of affection and acceptance from a man that the boy needs. These destructive words and actions when the boy is young can later cause him to gravitate to a homosexual lifestyle as he unconsciously searches for the male acceptance he never had as a child.

This boy grows up shaped by the rejection he experienced from his father. He has been taught that men don't hug or kiss — only "queers" kiss. Yet in his heart, he knows he just needs someone to give him a hug. Sadly, he may end up believing that the only hugs from a man he can get are the kind associated with sex.

A homosexual man once said to me, "You don't know what it is like to finally be accepted and hugged by a man after you've been rejected by your father your entire life. You can't know what it feels like to finally receive the acceptance you've always wanted."

Children need displays of affection from their parents. They need their parents to kiss them, hug them, and tell them how wonderful they are.

Dad, tell your son how strong he is and what a great man you believe he is going to become. Don't ever call your son a sissy or a baby, thinking that will bring out the strong man in him. What you're actually doing is challenging his manhood! And if you challenge that boy's manhood to a certain point, you can cause him to go over the edge and to act in a way that contradicts his manhood.

Now let's talk about young girls who are rejected by their fathers. Suppose a little girl experiences a lack of affection from her dad. He tells her often that she always does everything wrong. No matter how hard she tries, nothing she does seems to please him. After a while, the little girl turns inward. She doesn't want her father to hug her or kiss her anymore. She doesn't want to be "daddy's little girl" anymore. She becomes very cold.

As this girl grows older and passes through puberty, she begins to look for any male who will give her affection. She doesn't want to have sex; she wants affection. But she comes to believe that the only way she can get the affection she craves is by giving herself sexually to a man. This girl's promiscuity can be traced back to the destructive words and rejection of her childhood.

A person will most often go the path of least resistance. Therefore, this girl may end up as a prostitute, or she may marry the first man who shows her affection. Whichever direction she chooses, the girl's life has been dealt a death blow by the negative words and actions of her father.

From the Heart,
The Mouth Speaks

So where do our negative words come from, and how do we stop speaking them? It all has to do with the renovation of our minds.

Jesus talked about the origin of our words as He dealt with the religious legalists of His day. This is what Jesus said:

> **"Hypocrites! Well did Isaiah prophesy about you, saying:**
> **'These people draw near to Me with their mouth, and honor Me with their lips, but their heart is far from Me.**
> **And in vain they worship Me, teaching as doctrines the commandments of men.'"**
> **When He had called the multitude to Himself, He said to them, "Hear and understand:**
> **"Not what goes into the mouth defiles a man; but what comes out of the mouth, this defiles a man."**
>
> **Matthew 15:7-11**

Jesus called these religious leaders "hypocrites." The Greek word "hypocrite" essentially means *one who speaks from behind the mask.* Another translation of the word "hypocrite" is *pretender* — in other words, a person who pretends to be something he isn't.

Jesus called these men hypocrites because they were judging the disciples on how well they lived a righteous life according to the Law. Jesus responded in essence, "Listen, Isaiah did well when he prophesied about you, you hypocrites! Even though you're drawing near to Me with your mouth and honoring Me with your lips, your heart is far from Me.

"Don't you understand that what goes into a man's mouth is not what destroys him? That which enters a man's mouth is eventually eliminated and flushed away. What really matters in a person's life are the words that proceed *out of* a person's mouth, because those words come forth from his heart. They live on forever!"

Jesus' message here confirms Proverbs 23:7, which says, **"For as he thinks in his heart, so is he...."** What has been going on in *your* mind, my friend? As you think in your heart, so are you!

Then Jesus said, **"But those things which proceed out of the mouth come from the heart, and they defile a man"** (Matt. 15:18). The word "heart" here refers to your *motivation*. Your heart produces thoughts. Your thoughts produce words. Your words produce attitudes. And your attitudes produce actions. That's why the Bible says that as a man thinks in his heart, so is he! That's also why Jesus said that wrong thoughts, which produce wrong words, provide the poison that defiles the man.

If your thought life is out of control today, you are the one who allowed it to get that way. You can't blame it on anyone else. However, you are also the one who can change it!

You might say, "I just can't stop thinking and speaking this way. I just can't stop!"

That is a lie of the devil, and you have swallowed it! The truth is, you don't want to stop the way you're thinking. Otherwise, you *would* stop because it doesn't take any more time to think God's Word than it does to think the negative thoughts you've been thinking.

What Comes *Out* of a Man Defiles Him

I remember back when I was eighteen years old, I started to get into some pretty bad things in my life. At first, participating in those wrong activities didn't come easily to me. I had to read material about it before I was convinced enough to do it. Then I thought, *Well, this must all right. This must be the way everyone does it.*

From the moment I believed the material I had read, I accepted the sin it talked about as "okay." And from that moment on, that sin took control of me. I could no longer tell it "no" because I had nothing to replace it with. I couldn't get rid of the words that had entered my mind as I read that material. I saw them day after day after day after day. And because of those words planted in my mind, the sin I was committing seemed acceptable to me. Nevertheless, deep down within me, my sinful thoughts and actions were slowly killing me.

That's what Jesus meant when He said, "It isn't what goes into a man that defiles him, but what comes *out*." Then he said, **"For out of the heart proceed evil thoughts, murders, adulteries, fornications, thefts, false witness, blasphemies"** (Matt. 15:19).

You see, adultery doesn't start with a person's body; it starts in his *brain*. The religious leaders who challenged Jesus felt very holy despite the perverted thoughts in their minds. They could always use the excuse, "So what if I thought about committing adultery? I never did it!"

But Jesus wouldn't let them get away with their hypocrisy. He said, "You guys are pretenders! You keep the external commandments you want to keep, but your hearts are far from Me!" These religious legalists just loved to look a particular way, but the one thing they never dealt with was their own hearts and minds. According to their hypocritical standard, they could entertain negative thoughts if they wanted to. They could be as perverted or covetous as they wanted to be inside their minds. Then they'd say, "It's all right because I never did it."

So Jesus told these religious hypocrites:

"You have heard that it was said to those of old, 'You shall not commit adultery.'
"But I say to you that whoever looks at a woman to lust for her has already committed adultery with her in his heart."

Matthew 5:27,28

If a man's purpose in looking at a woman is to lust after her in his thoughts, he has already committed adultery. It's already done.

You may ask, "Well, then, why don't I just go ahead and commit the physical act of adultery since I'm already guilty of committing the sin in my heart?" *Because whatever you do to your body will ultimately control your mind.*

That's why it's so important to stop sin in its thought stage. Once you commit sin with your body, it's much, much more difficult to deal with it and to get it out of your life for good. That's true no matter what the sin is. Adultery is just the example Jesus used.

Your Words
Reflect Your Relationship With God

The *Johnson* translation of Matthew 12:33-35 gives us further insight into the importance of the words we think and speak. Our words actually reflect the quality of our relationship with God![6]

Either get your life in union with God and let your behavior demonstrate that, or else let your life get completely out of control and your behavior will reflect that. A person's inner life is recognized by his behavior.

So many of you listening to me are self-deluded pretenders. When you are out of union with God, how can you talk

---

[6] Ben Campbell Johnson, *Matthew and Mark: A Relational Paraphrase* (Waco, Texas: Word Books, 1978), pp. 47-48.

about that which is good? Don't you realize that the words which come out of your mouth express your innermost being?

If a person's behavior is good, it is because he is drawing out of the inner life of union with God. If a person's behavior is destructive, it is likewise because he is acting from a distorted or confused relationship with God.

Your actions are either a result of a healthy relationship with God or of a distorted, confused relationship with Him. And the main thing that determines the condition of that relationship is your thought life and the words that come out of your mouth.

You see, my friend, every word you speak is an indicator of how it is between you and God — and for this, you are accountable. The direction you point your words is the outcome you will produce in your life. Your words will either point toward your wholeness, or they will point toward your destruction. And once those words are spoken, the power contained within them cannot be stopped.

Let's look at an example on the positive side. If you decide you're going to be healed according to the Word and you begin to continually speak God's healing promises in faith, no devil in hell can stop you from being healed. If you've made up your mind to believe the Word, God Himself can't stop you because He has already said it. And once He has said something, He is not going to turn back on it!

God will never supercede His own Word. Numbers 23:19 confirms this:

"God is not a man, that He should lie, nor a son of man, that He should repent. Has He said, and will He not do? Or has He spoken, and will He not make it good?"

God will make good whatever you *believe* and *speak* according to His Word.

Don't Let the Devil Talk You Out of Victory!

Even though I fill my mind with thoughts of God's Word on a continual basis, my mind can still be a battlefield. The devil tries to insert all sorts of thoughts into my mind that don't have anything to do with the Word. If I'm not careful, I can almost talk myself out of believing the Word of God based on my natural feelings. Thank God, I don't fall for the devil's strategies, but it's a mental battle I often face.

The enemy is just as interested in defeating *you* on the battlefield of your mind. For example, he loves to talk to you right after you pray about something.

Before you prayed, you were doing fine. You meditated on the Word for weeks, and you knew for sure God was going to give it to you. You thought, *Oh, glory, thank You, Jesus. I have my answer in Jesus' Name!* Then you said, "Amen," and immediately the thought shot through your mind: *You're a loser, pal.*

All the devil is trying to do is get you to say with your own mouth that it isn't going to work. So his thoughts start bombarding your mind: *It's not going to work. It's not going to work. It's not going to work. It's not going to work.* If you don't replace those thoughts with God's promises, they will torment you until you suddenly blurt out, "You know what? It's not going to work!"

Once you say those words, your mind isn't bothered anymore with those tormenting thoughts. Why? Because after you prayed to receive your answer, you gave it away with your words. And as soon as you gave it away, the devil just said, *"Thank you! Bye bye!"*

Are you beginning to understand the power contained in your words?

Make Your Mind Think God's Thoughts

Did you know you can *allow* your mind to think negative thoughts, or you can *make* your mind think God's thoughts? It is a lazy person who just lets any thought the devil sends his way set up residence in his mind.

People often say to me, "But you just don't know what I'm going through. You just don't know how hard it is for me."

I know those people are just like everyone else. Every person is tempted to their own level of spirituality and to the extent they allow the devil to plant his thoughts in their minds. You see, all day long the devil just keeps taking away whatever a person won't fight him for.

So when people say to me, "Yeah, but you just don't know how I feel," I answer, "Yes, I do, because it is obvious you're letting the devil's thoughts run rampant in your mind. You feel crummy. You're losing. You think that it's just about all over for you. You think you're close to giving up. You think you're some kind of special case. You think God has passed you by and that He doesn't really care anymore."

The truth is, you never have to allow your mind to think all those lies. Remember, Proverbs 12:5 says, **"The thoughts of the righteous are right, but the counsels of the wicked are deceitful."** Therefore, you can *make* your mind think, *I'm righteous, and I think right thoughts. I'm righteous, and I think right thoughts.*

The devil tries again: *"You know something? Your boss is out to destroy you!"*

I'm righteous, and I think right thoughts.

"You're going to go down the tubes. Do you understand that?"

I'm righteous, and I think right thoughts.

All of a sudden, the mental torment stops — at least for the moment. At that point, you can go on to something else. For instance, you can meditate on God's precious promise found in Second Corinthians 5:21: *He who knew no sin was made to be sin for me so I could be made the righteousness of God in Him.*

The devil may try a new tactic: *"You haughty thing, you!"*

He who knew no sin was made to be sin for me so I could be made the righteousness of God in Him.

"Look at your life. How can you say you're righteous?"

He who knew no sin was made to be sin for me so I could be made the righteousness of God in Him. According to Colossians 1:22, I am holy, unblameable, unaccusable, and unreproveable without fault or failure in my Father's sight!

"Yeah, but look at what you did."

I am unaccusable in the Name of Jesus. I'm unaccusable. I'm unaccusable!

As you make your mind think God's thoughts, you'll begin to know how to respond to difficult situations you face in life. For example, I remember an incident back when Linda and I were young in ministry. It was a great time for us as we learned how to apply our lives to the Word. But we also learned that some people want to manipulate and control others with their attitudes. They try to "put the screws" on people with the things they say.

One day that happened to Linda. A woman came up to her and said, "You don't care about people. You don't care about anything but your religion!"

Now, you have to stretch a long way to tell Linda she doesn't care about people! But regardless, you'll never convince Linda of that.

This person just kept reading Linda the absolute riot act, spouting off a torrent of critical words. Finally, Linda just stopped her and said, "Excuse me. I just want to tell you something. I'm holy, unblameable, unaccusable, and unreproveable."

When this woman heard that, she got so mad that she almost had steam rising from her face! She spun around and stomped off in a huff. But the next afternoon, she called Linda and said, "You know something? I need to ask you to forgive me. You were right, and I was wrong."

You see, you can either be controlled, or you can allow God's Word to control you!

Paint a Picture of Success In Your Heart

Let's talk further about how your words affect your life. In Joshua 1:8, it says this:

"This Book of the Law shall not depart from your mouth, but you shall meditate in it day and night, that you may observe to do according to all that is written in it. For then you will make your way prosperous, and then you will have good success."

God reveals an important principle here that can help us in the renovation of our minds. However, this principle can cut both ways, both positive and negative.

First, He said, **"This Book of the Law shall not depart from your mouth, but you shall meditate**

in it day and night...." Let's substitute "this Book of the Law" with one of the devil's "books," such as "this book of sickness" or "this book of poverty" or "this book of unrighteousness." If a person meditates on one of those devilish books day and night and talks about it all the time, it begins to paint a picture of defeat in his mind.

That person starts saying things like, "I'm tellin' you, Mabel, as sure as shootin', as soon as we decide we're going to go on a vacation, all the kids are going to get sick. It happens every time." Then when all the kids get sick, he says, "See, I told you so!" He may even be proud that he was accurate in his predictions!

Or he might say to his wife, "Well, let's go down to the car lot and buy that new car. But I bet you that as soon as we buy it, I'll get laid off my job!" So he buys the new car. Sure enough, a few days later he gets laid off his job. He comes home and says to his wife, "See, I told you so!"

Why do that person's words come to pass? Because he has meditated on the words of a devilish "book," and he hasn't let those words depart from his mouth. Therefore, the Bible says he will begin to observe to do according to all that is written in that book of defeat!

This principle works whether you're meditating on the Word or on negative thoughts of sickness, poverty, and defeat. You see, you don't think in words; you think in pictures. Therefore, the thoughts you dwell on in your mind will determine the pictures that are painted within you. And those inner pictures will determine what direction you go in life.

Proverbs 29:18 (*NAS*) says, **"Where there is no vision, the people are unrestrained...."** The vision you are developing inside your mind through the thoughts you think will eventually manifest in your life either for good or for bad. If you have been meditating on sinful things, it is like lighting a long fuse on an M80 firecracker. As you keep looking at those negative inner pictures, one day — *boom!* you speak them out and then act on them.

Then you say, "Look at what I just did! I can't believe I did this!" You might even try to blame your sin on God, as many people do when they mess up. As Proverbs 19:3 (*NLT*) says, **"People ruin their lives by their own foolishness and then are angry at the Lord."**[7]

But how long had you been thinking about doing what you did?

"Oh, I've been thinking about it for a couple of months."

And you couldn't stop it in two months?

"I just didn't know how to stop it!"

How you stop wrong thoughts is simple: *You make God's Word your thought pattern.*

As you pattern your thoughts after God's Word, you begin to paint pictures on the inside that reflect

---

[7] *New Living Translation*, p. 1005.

God's will for you. These pictures will cause you to **"...observe to do according to all that is written in it. For then you will make your way prosperous, and then you will have good success."** You will prosper and experience success in life when the picture you're seeing in your heart is in line with the Word of God.

That's why I keep stressing that what you think determines the outcome of your life. This is the way it works:

- What you think causes you to speak certain words.

- What you speak paints pictures in your heart.

- And the inner pictures you paint determine your direction and ultimate destiny in life.

Change the Pictures Of Your Past

So what is the difference between a winner or a loser in life? *The loser never changes the pictures he has already painted.* For instance, I was talking to a relative recently about his life. He told me, "You know, if I really thought obeying the Word of God was going to help my life, I'd do it."

I said, "How is your eyesight? I mean, just compare your life to mine. You and I are no different. We have the same background. We went through the same things. We have the same feelings. Yet you're failing, and I'm not.

"Let me tell you why that is tru
thinking about what happened when
ing up, and I gave that up long ago. '
difference between us. I gave up the l
the shame, the degradation — all the things uuu
were adversely determining my future. The day I
got born again, October 28, 1975, was the day Robb
Thompson died. He no longer lives.

"All those bad things that happened to me before
I was born again don't mean a thing to me now. As
far as I'm concerned, they happened to someone
else. They are nothing but faint memories to me.
The old things that don't belong to my new life in
Christ have all passed away, and I'm living a new
life in Him!"

Now, let me add a note of caution here. Many
Christians have meditated on and confessed the
Word for hours and hours and yet never received
any benefit from it. Why is that? Because they never
mixed faith with what they were meditating on!

These believers didn't hold fast to the promise
when the devil put pressure on them. They didn't
stick with what was written. Rather than continuing to put pressure on God's Word, they gave in to
the enemy's pressure, allowing his thoughts to beat
up their minds and push them toward certain
defeat.

You have to keep putting pressure on the Word of
God inside you, my friend. As you do that, it will
always work for you because God is absolutely faithful to His Word, and He is no respecter of persons.

so stick with the Word at all costs. Remember that whatever you put into your heart is what you're going to get out of it. You see, the Word of God is like an egg with a very hard shell that you hold in your hand. When you squeeze that egg, it doesn't break easily. But if you'll just keep squeezing, eventually it will break and you'll get the gooey prize inside!

The same is true with God's Word. As you keep meditating on the Word and speaking it forth with your mouth, the day will come when the "shell" is cracked and the prize is won. Someone may just mention a verse to you — when suddenly the revelation of that scripture hits your heart and changes your life forever!

My friend, the day has to come in your life when you are finally fed up with all the death-dealing words you have allowed to run through your mind and come forth from your mouth. Do those words define the outcome you want for your life? If your answer is *"No!"* then understand this: You can stop thinking and speaking those words anytime you want to by obeying Joshua 1:8.

Meditate on God's Word day and night. Speak forth those life-giving words with your mouth. Paint pictures on the inside that help you observe to do what is written. As the words you think and speak become containers of *life* and *hope* rather than self-made coffins of *death* and *defeat*, the results will be obvious — you'll begin to prosper and have good success in every area of life!

7

ELIMINATING CONFUSION FROM YOUR LIFE

In discussing how to acquire "saved brains," I've spent quite a bit of time nailing down some basic, vital scriptural principles. In order to renovate your mind, you must identify with Christ in His death, burial, and resurrection. You must understand your righteousness in Christ. You must let go of your past. And you must recognize and harness the power in your words.

Why have I stressed these points so much? Because one of the biggest obstacles people face in renewing their minds is *confusion*. They are unable to distinguish between right and wrong because they are ignorant of the Word. Therefore, their minds remain trapped in a maze of destructive thought patterns that make it difficult for them to make good decisions in life.

That's why I want to talk to you about how you can eliminate confusion from your life. First, let's see what James has to say about this subject of confusion:

> **Who is a wise man and endued with knowledge among you? let him shew out of a good conversation his works with meekness of wisdom.**
> **But if ye have bitter envying and strife in your hearts, glory not, and lie not against the truth.**
> **This wisdom descendeth not from above, but is earthly, sensual, devilish.**
> **FOR WHERE ENVYING AND STRIFE IS, THERE IS CONFUSION AND EVERY EVIL WORK.**
>
> **James 3:13-16 (*KJV*)**

In this passage of Scripture, James is dealing with a set of people who have a party spirit. A person with a party spirit gathers a lot of people around himself who agree with him at the exclusion of others who *don't* agree. In this case, James is talking about some false teachers who were twisting the Word of God for their own gain (*see* James 3:1). These false teachers wanted something from the people, and they twisted God's Word in order to obtain it.

So James asks, **"Who is a wise man and endued with knowledge among you?..."** (v. 13 *KJV*). In other words, he is saying, "Look, you can't just use knowledge when you teach God's Word. Your ability to put out knowledge is not all God wants for His people. You must actually impart *wisdom* to people — that which is gleaned after knowledge is obtained."

You see, God wanted His people to receive revelation from the teaching of the Scriptures, but these men had none. They were actually twisting and wresting the Scriptures to their own destruction.

James goes on to say, **"...Let him shew out of a good conversation** [or manner of life] **his works with meekness of wisdom"** (v. 13 *KJV*). This word "meekness" here refers to the ability to take correction without lashing back at the person who gives it. This is an important quality because anyone who teaches others about the Word of God is not in a position to protect himself from people.

A teacher must love the people he ministers to even when they're fighting him the entire time. He has to go in to rescue a person out of the snare of the devil even when that person is criticizing him behind his back or saying, "I hate you!" the entire time. And the teacher has to do it all without taking into account a wrong suffered!

Then in verse 14 (*KJV*), it says, **"But if ye have bitter envying and strife in your hearts, glory not, and lie not against the truth."** When a person desires what someone else has and tries to compete for it, that is a sign he has bitter envy and strife in his heart. This type of person doesn't like it when he sees someone else get in front of him spiritually. Feelings of strife and envy begin to rub him raw on the inside.

James says to that person, "Glory not. Don't boast about the things you have or the things you want. And lie not against the Word of God because it has now come to convict you."

James goes on to say, **"This wisdom descendeth not from above, but is earthly, sensual, devilish"** (v. 15 *KJV*). Actually, this is the way the world runs. This wisdom of "giving to get"; "I want what you have"; "more is better"; and "gain is godliness" is earthly and caters to a person's natural senses. James even calls this type of wisdom *devilish*!

Where Does Confusion Come From?

Verse 16 (*KJV*) is the key scripture that helps us understand where confusion comes from. It says, **"For where envying and strife is, there is confusion and every evil work."** According to this verse, confusion — which includes disturbance, trouble, and instability — originates in a person's fierce desire to promote his own selfish opinion.

God will never be party to that type of selfish promotion. He does not promote your opinions at the exclusion of others. Besides, no one can keep you from being promoted if you deserve it. When you are faithful, you always rise to the top.

Remember, confusion is the inability to distinguish between right and wrong. One reason we get into this kind of confusion is that we go after the things the world has to offer with our faith. We begin to compete in faith with others rather than believing God's Word because of our love for Him.

Your faith life is not horizontal; it is *vertical*. You never need to look down the line to find out what someone else's faith is producing in his life. Also, you should never say things like, "Well, I'm believing God for a car, and that person has an extra car sitting in the driveway. So I'll just ask the Lord to touch that person's heart and cause him to give me that car." That isn't wisdom from above; it's devilish. In fact, it gets dangerously close to what could be called "Charismatic witchcraft"!

If God really wanted that person to give you the car, why didn't He tell him? You just need to stay away from that kind of praying because it really isn't "faith." It is actually a selfish desire for self-promotion and gain that leads to **"...confusion and every evil work."**

Only Two Voices

Let's take this question of what causes people to become confused a little further. One thing many Christians get confused about is where their wrong thoughts come from. They say, "My old self tells me I want to do the bad things I used to do before I was saved. I know those thoughts must have come from my old self because God didn't tell me to do that." These believers assume there are three voices in the world: the voice of the Holy Spirit, who leads and guides them; the devil's voice, who tries to get them off track; and their own voice.

I can clear up that confusion right now. Don't get the idea for one moment that there are three voices in the world — God, the devil, and you. There are only two voices, not three, and you're listening to one or the other all the time. There are thoughts that originate from God and thoughts that originate out of Satan's kingdom. Which voice you heed in your mind at any given moment depends on what you are believing at that moment.

Don't think for a moment that you are a special entity who lives outside the control of God or the devil. There isn't one original thought on the face of this earth. You haven't thought anything original in your entire life. Your thoughts are influenced either by God or by the devil at all times.

You are also not the only person who is going through what you're going through right now, However, the devil wants you to think you are. He wants to tell you, *God doesn't love you because of what is going on inside your mind. God is jumping your case. He's going to judge you! It's all over for you because of what you've been thinking.*

No, it's just *beginning* for you because you're learning how to renovate your mind!

Stopping the Progression
From Thought to Sin

Satan likes to keep us confused about whose thoughts we're listening to in our minds. That makes it easier for us to progress from just listening to a *thought* to committing a *sin*.

However, you can learn how to tell which thoughts come from Satan's kingdom. For instance, suppose you're going through life having a wonderful time with Jesus when suddenly the thought comes to your mind: *You want to take some drugs, don't you?*

You think to yourself, *I wonder why I'm starting to have this desire to take drugs. Christians don't have thoughts about taking drugs. What's wrong with me?*

Another thought comes: *Hey, come on, let's go do something. Come on, let's take some drugs!* All of a sudden, you're feeling pressure.

No, you're not schizophrenic. You don't think good thoughts and bad thoughts at the same time. Remember, your old self has been crucified with Christ. Your flesh is up on the cross. That's just the devil talking to you, trying to convince you to pull your flesh off the cross so it can do as it pleases!

But if you don't realize which voice is talking to you, you might start listening to those thoughts. You might start thinking, *Well, what's really wrong with doing drugs? I'm free. I can do whatever I want. All things are lawful for me, and I'm not going to hurt anyone with it, so what's so wrong with it?*

All of a sudden, you begin to believe that you want to do drugs. And once you believe that's what you want to do, faith comes. In other words, you put your faith in wanting to sin rather than in wanting to obey God's Word. At that moment, you release your flesh to come off the cross and lead you through the mud and grime of sin.

So the next time the enemy inserts a thought in your mind, telling you that you want to sin, remember this: Nothing comes into your mind that you *must* do. Once you figure that out, then no matter what the devil says you want to do, you won't do it anymore. You'll just tell him, "No, I'm not going to do that!"

Of course, the day you tell the devil no is the day his attack gets even more intense. He'll say to your mind, *Yes, but you want to do it. You want it!* Don't listen to him. If you do, you might start asking yourself questions and crying to yourself, *What is wrong with me? Why do I want to do this?*

You *don't* want to do it. All you want to do is serve God. But the enemy is coming to your mind in your own voice and telling you otherwise!

So this is how you deal with the devil when he speaks to your mind. He says, *Come on, you want to go do some drugs?* He waits for your reply and hears nothing.

Come on, let's go get loaded. Come on, let's go commit adultery. Come on, let's walk away from God. No answer. *Why aren't you talking to me? Come on, I'm talking to you!*

The devil is getting the same response from you that you would get from a corpse in a casket if you tried to talk to it. No matter how much you talk to that corpse, it isn't moving!

It's exactly the same with you when the devil talks to your mind. All you need to do is first recognize who is talking to you. Then hold fast to the truth that you are the righteousness of God in Christ Jesus. Finally, determine never to move one inch just because the devil tells you to!

Four Biblical Words for 'Mind'

In the interest of eliminating every source of confusion as we renovate our minds, let's talk about what the Bible means by the word "mind." The fact is, there are four major words in the New Testament used for the word "mind." The first one is the word *nous*; the second is the word *dianoia*; the third is *phronema*; and the fourth is *phroneo*.

As we look at these four Greek words, we will see that each one represents a stage in the process of gaining control of our minds. First, I'll give you the definition of these words; then we'll go back to each one and discuss it further.

- The word *nous* refers to *your thoughts, your feelings, and your will.*[8] Actually, it is *your thinking power.*[9]

- The word *dianoia* refers to *deep thought* or *the mind's disposition, imagination, and understanding.*[10]

- The third word, *phronema*, means *to have an inclination and a purpose.*[11]

- Finally, *phroneo* means *to entertain or have sentiment towards;*[12] *to set one's affections upon.*[13]

Now, notice the stages of renovating the mind. At first, we deal with just our thoughts and our will, or our thinking power. That affects our deep thoughts and imaginations — those inner pictures we talked about earlier. Third, we come to a place where we have an inclination — a purpose and a direction. Finally, we set our affections upon that purpose, allowing it to consume our strength, energy, and attention.

The First Stage:
Renewing the Mind (*Nous*)

Let's deal with the word *nous* first. First, Romans 1:28 speaks of the negative side of *nous*, describing

---

[8] James Strong, "Greek Dictionary of the New Testament," *The Strong's Exhaustive Concordance of the Bible* (McLean, Virginia: MacDonald Publishing Co.), p. 50, #3563.
[9] Reinecker and Rogers, p. 375.
[10] Strong, p. 22, #1271.
[11] Ibid., p. 76, #5427.
[12] Ibid., p. 76, #5426.
[13] Reinecker and Rogers, p. 365.

what happens to people who refuse to acknowledge God in their lives:

And even as they did not like to retain God in their knowledge, God gave them over to a debased mind, to do those things which are not fitting.

Notice it says, **"...they did not like to retain God in their knowledge...."** That means they put God to the test and then made their decision to turn aside from Him. So God turned them over to a debased or reprobate mind (*nous*).

These people no longer had any inclinations or thoughts concerning God. God had become the furthest thing from their minds. They no longer retained Him in their thoughts and in the exercise of their will. They burned in lust, man for man and woman for woman.

They actually refused to worship God, even though they knew He was God. They didn't treat Him or honor Him as God, nor were they thankful. Instead, they became vain in their imaginations, and their foolish hearts were darkened (*see* Romans 1:18-32).

Another scripture using the word *nous* is in Romans 7:23. Paul relates the very real struggle a person can go through in his mind (*nous*) as he battles against the desires of the flesh. When I was first born again, I went through the very thing Paul describes.

As you know, I was born again in a mental institution in 1975. But all my mental battles didn't end as soon as I got born again. Before I was saved, I had five conversations going on in my head at once. Afterwards, I still had two!

One voice told me I wanted to do what was right, and the other one told me I didn't. I wasn't really sure what I wanted to do because the one that kept telling me I wanted to do wrong was louder than the other one that told me I wanted to do right.

Over and over again, I'd retreat to my walk-in closet to repent, my head pounding from the intense mental struggle. I didn't understand why I kept wanting to do what God didn't want me to do. Obviously, I still had a lot to learn!

This is what the man is going through in Romans 7:23. Paul describes the struggle:

But I see another law in my members, warring against the law of my mind, and bringing me into captivity to the law of sin which is in my members.

That term "warring" means that these thoughts had conducted a military expedition against this man's mind. They actually began to stalk him and oppose his mind with stratagems of deceit and lies.

The same is true for you. Right now, your mind is being stalked by evil. You are actually being studied by the prince of darkness so he can find a way to trick you into believing what he has to say.

Paul goes on to say that the demonic military expedition that had ambushed this man's mind was actually bringing him into captivity. The word "captivity" here means *to capture with a spear*.[14] So in a sense, these thoughts captured the man with a spear and took him as a prisoner of war in his own mind. Instead of this person taking his thoughts captive, he was taken captive by his thoughts! Once in captivity, his will became involved as he chose to do what he knew was wrong.

Then the man says in verse 24, **"O wretched man that I am!..."** (As I said before, there is nothing more miserable than a Christian out of fellowship with God!) **"...Who will deliver me from this body of death?"** This man was convinced that his body was running his life as Satan waged this intense military onslaught against him in his members, in his mind, and in his thought patterns.

Satan had practiced watching this man the same way Satan practices watching *you*. The enemy will try to wait for the opportune time to get you to believe what he wants you to believe; then he'll bombard your mind with one negative thought after another. And as long as you listen to his thoughts, he has a fair chance of taking you captive whenever he desires.

You see, Satan never has to bother a person who isn't believing God's Word. That's why it's easy to get confused when you look at unsaved people who seem happy. You think, *I know those people. They never hear anyone preach the Word to them, yet*

---

[14] Ibid., p. 364.

they're just so happy! They're carnal, but they're happy. Their jobs are going great, and everything seems to be going all right for them. I just can't figure out why they're so happy!

The reason things are going so smooth for these people is that the devil knows he can take them whenever he wants them. Therefore, he leaves them alone for now because they are making absolutely no waves in his kingdom.

The day you decide to believe the Word of God is the day you put a big, invisible bulls'-eye on your back. Why is that? Because all that time you weren't believing God, Satan had no reason to bother you. You were doing quite well at destroying your own life with the words of your mouth!

But then comes the day you start saying things like, "The Word of God says that by the stripes of Jesus, I'm healed!" All of a sudden, the devil sits up and takes notice. He says, "What? Well, we'll have to fix this little problem. Flu, go after him! Sickness and disease, launch an attack!"

Then the devil stands before God every chance he gets to accuse you. He says, "So-and-so stumbled in his confession of faith today. He said these words of doubt and unbelief. Therefore, by the words of his mouth I have the right of access to his life!"

Meanwhile, you're thinking, *I thought this stuff about believing God was the truth. Man, oh, man, ever since I started believing God, all hell has broken loose in my life!*

That may very well be true. But you just need to "batten down the hatches" and ride the storm like a ship on a big wave. It's going to take some time to clean out all those negative thoughts and renew your mind with God's Word. But once you've established the habit of thinking and talking the Word in every situation, Satan's strategies against you will be thwarted every time!

Finally, let's look one more time at Romans 12:2, which gives us the positive side of the word *nous*:

And do not be conformed to this world, but be transformed by the renewing of your mind, that you may prove what is that good and acceptable and perfect will of God.

I just want to point out here that the phrase "renewing of the mind" (*nous*) is speaking of a *continual* renewing. You have to continue at all times to renew your mind with the Word of God. You never "arrive" nor come to a place in this life where your mind is completely renewed.

You are continually evolving into who God's Word says you are, so work on renovating your mind every day. No matter how renewed your mind is at this moment, it isn't as renewed as it is going to be because you are never going to stop moving on with God!

The Second Stage:
Dealing With the Deeper Stains of Sin

Now let's talk about the second Greek word, *dianoia*, that is translated "mind" in the Bible.

Remember, *dianoia* refers to our deep thoughts, our disposition, our imagination, and our understanding.

In Ephesians 2:2,3 (*KJV*), it says this:

Wherein in time past ye walked according to the course of this world, according to the prince of the power of the air, the spirit that now worketh in the children of disobedience:

Among whom also we all had our conversation in times past in the lusts of our flesh, fulfilling the desires of the flesh and of the mind; and were by nature the children of wrath, even as others.

The word "conversation" in verse 3 is talking about our social actions or outward conduct that once ran contrary to the ways of God. Paul was saying, "Before you were born again, the whole world could see that you were not in union with God."

Verse 3 goes on to say that our past conduct was based **"...in the lusts of our flesh, fulfilling the desires of the flesh and of the mind...."** This word "mind" here is the word *dianoia*. So Paul is saying that we began to fulfill the desires of our flesh and of *our deep thoughts and disposition*. In other words, those fleshly desires were no longer just a few thoughts running through our minds. They had become deep thoughts that had gotten down on the inside of us and affected our disposition.

Once the lusts of the flesh and of the mind reach this stage, they are much more difficult to deal with. Even after we are born again, we may still struggle to be free of these deep-seated thoughts once and for all.

If you're going through this kind of struggle, you might think, *How am I ever going to change in this area? It seems like that sinful desire never goes away. It just wants to hold on and never let go. How am I ever really going to get rid of it? I've been speaking God's Word for six months, yet over and over again, I still get dragged back into doing something I don't want to do.*

But remember this, my friend: *You can't crucify a demon, and you cannot cast out the flesh.* Yes, your old nature was changed to a new nature through the new birth, but you still have your flesh. You won't get anywhere saying, "You foul cigarettes, I command you to take your hands off me" or "Beer bottle, in Jesus' Name, I command you to loose me!" No beer bottle ever holds you — you hold *it!* You have to *choose* to keep that flesh up on the cross!

Some people want to take the easy road out of their problem, so they attribute all their fleshly desires to demons. With a glass of alcohol in their hand, they say, "You foul demon of drinking (gulp, gulp, gulp), let me go in Jesus' Name!"

You know, I wish every problem *was* the result of a demon. Then we could have a mass deliverance service and make everyone perfect all at once! I'd just say, *"Come out* in Jesus' Name," and everyone would be set free! Then Jesus could return for us that same night because we would be ready for Him — without one spot, blemish, or wrinkle!

But it doesn't work that way. Even though we are born again, we still have to deal with the flesh. It doesn't go away. And the only way we can ever deal with the flesh effectively is by continually renewing our minds (*nous*) through the washing of the water of the Word.

Now, some of us have deeper stains than others. Therefore, in order to get deep enough to make those stains go away, we have to stay very diligent in washing our minds with the Word.

You see, fleshly strongholds that have settled deep in your *dianoia* don't go away just because you want them to. In fact, the more you think about the sin that has held you in bondage over the years, the worse your mental struggle gets. Your mind becomes consumed with thoughts of self-condemnation as you think over and over, *I hate it. I hate it. I hate it!*

Why don't you just judge yourself according to the Word of God and then forget about it? Stop condemning yourself over the matter all the time; instead, focus on what *God* says about it. He promises that **"...if we would judge ourselves, we would not be judged"** (1 Cor. 11:31).

As long as you're on this earth, you still have to deal with your flesh. It doesn't go away no matter what you do. Your flesh is there, and it's going to be there until you go home to be with Jesus. So do the one thing you can do about it — never stop renewing your mind through the washing of the water of the Word!

No Longer an Enemy of God In Your Mind (*Dianoia*)

Colossians 1:21,22 also translates the word *dianoia* as the word "mind":

And you, who once were alienated and enemies in your mind by wicked works, yet now He has reconciled
in the body of His flesh through death, to present you holy, and blameless, and above reproach in His sight.

The word "alienated" in verse 21 means that we were formerly *estranged* from God, settled in our minds that we were against Him and that He was against us. We were enemies of God in our *dianoia*, or in our deep thoughts, before we received Him.

However, some believers are still enemies of God in their deep thoughts, imaginations, and inner pictures. What causes them to remain enemies of God deep down on the inside? Verse 21 tells us it is *by wicked works*.

In certain areas of their lives, these people have developed negative attitudes toward God. And when they hear what the Word has to say about these areas, a bitterness against God rears up within them. If left unchecked, that bitterness can actually cause them to become God's enemy in the deep recesses of their minds.

That is why it is so important to completely divorce ourselves from everything in this world except the Cross of Christ. That should be our only link to this world because it gives us our divine purpose. We are here on this earth for two reasons: number one, to be blessed by God and to proclaim His glory; and number two, to preach the Gospel to every creature.

None of us should remain at enmity with God in our deep thoughts and imaginations. God has provided a clear way for us to be presented before Him **"...holy and unblameable and unreproveable in his sight"** (v. 22 *KJV*). That provision is stated in verse 23:

If indeed you continue in the faith, grounded and steadfast, AND ARE NOT MOVED AWAY FROM THE HOPE OF THE GOSPEL which you heard....

Never allow yourself to be moved away from the Word of God. Stick to that which is written no matter what is going on around you.

You might say, "Boy, you stress this one point a lot!" And I'll keep stressing it until you get it! Why? Because I know that once you do get it — once you begin thinking, speaking, and doing the Word in every situation — it will eliminate all confusion in your mind and stop the endless cycle of strife and defeat in your life!

Notice that verse 23 says we are not to be moved away from **"...the hope of the gospel...."** That's exactly what the Bible is: *hope*. All we have to do is say, "God, whatever You say is mine in the Word, I claim it right now!"

When God hears that, He says, "Come and get it, child! It's yours. You don't need to do anything to get it. You don't need to become right in My sight because I have already made you blameless and unreproachable before Me."

I've known some people who did some abominable things before the Lord in the past. But when they testified, "You know, I'm believing God that I'm the righteousness of God in Christ Jesus," I couldn't condemn them for a moment. I just kept preaching the Word of God that they were the righteousness of God, and ultimately, they were set free!

You never help a person get set free by telling him how horrible he is and how bad the sins were that he committed. He already knows he is a failure as far as God is concerned. So instead of emphasizing what a person has done wrong, tell him God has made him *right* in His eyes. He is no longer an enemy of God in his mind — he is now the righteousness of God in Christ!

Carnally Minded vs. Spiritually Minded

After we deal with our deep thoughts and imaginations, we must come to terms with where we incline our affections, represented by the Greek word *phronema*. This is the word that is translated "mind" in Romans 8:6,7:

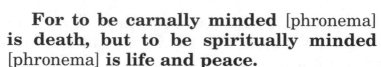
> **For to be carnally minded** [phronema] **is death, but to be spiritually minded** [phronema] **is life and peace.**
>
> **Because the carnal mind** [phronema] **is enmity against God; for it is not subject to the law of God, nor indeed can be.**

The "carnal mind" (*phronema*) refers to the person who first inclines himself toward carnality. He then makes it his purpose to set his affections on or to *mind* (*phroneo*) the things of the flesh (Rom. 8:5), regressing from just having an inclination toward sinful things to actually *desiring* those things. The flesh becomes the realm where his affections lie and where he spends his time and energy.

The carnally minded person is an enemy of God because he never places himself under the rule of God's Word. He is living according to his natural mind here on this earth, unwilling to subject himself or bow his knee to what the Word of God has to say about any given subject.

This person's opinions mean more to him than what God says about a situation. He rejects what God's Word has to say in favor of what the world has to offer. For instance, when God's Word says he becomes righteous by believing in Jesus Christ, his mind says, *I don't believe that. I believe I'm righteous by what I do.* When the Word of God says he is rich by virtue of believing in Jesus Christ, his mind says, *I don't believe that. I get rich by working hard.*

That's why it is ludicrous for a person to attempt to receive deliverance from God while he still has his affections set on the things of this world. As long as he is carnally minded, he can never subject himself to the law of God. Verse 8 says it this way: **"So then, those who are in the flesh cannot please God."**

Those who live in the flesh — who desire and have set their affections on the things of the flesh — cannot please God. Why? Because without faith, it is impossible to please Him (Heb. 11:6).

This person has absolutely no desire to believe in the provision Jesus has given to him through His death on the Cross. Instead, the person's desires, inclinations, and affections are set on the things he can get on his own. He's going to get all he can, and no one is going to stop him!

Don't let yourself be like that person. God warns that to be carnally minded is *death*. In other words, to be more interested in the things of this world than in the things of God produces death in your life.

On the other hand, to be spiritually minded produces life and peace. That's what Philippians 4:8 is talking about when it says this:

Finally, brethren, whatever things are true, whatever things are noble, whatever things are just, whatever things are pure, whatever things are lovely, whatever things are of good report, if there is any virtue and if there is anything praiseworthy — meditate on these things.

If your mind is consumed with thoughts that are contrary to the Word of God, those thoughts create a process that works death in your body, in your soul, and in every area of your life. On the other hand, when you set your mind on the things of God, you reap a harvest of life and peace.

Isaiah 26:3 (*KJV*) confirms this same principle:

Thou wilt keep him in perfect peace, whose mind is stayed on thee: because he trusteth in thee.

We don't trust in what we feel. We don't trust in what's going on inside our minds. We trust only in *God* and His Word.

Don't Listen to Any Voice That Contradicts the Word

If the thoughts running through my mind don't go along with the Word of God, I don't trust them. In fact, I immediately reject them because I know those thoughts don't come from me. I'm righteous in Christ, and, as we already found out, the thoughts of the righteous are only right (Prov. 12:5)!

This is how I look at it: Ephesians 2:6 tells me that God raised me up together and made me sit together in the heavenly places in Christ Jesus. Therefore, I am certainly not going to turn my back on God's Word so I can walk in the counsel of the ungodly, stand in the way of sinners, or sit in the seat of the scornful (Ps. 1:1)!

I'm going to be like that man in Psalm 1:2 who sets his affection on the Word of God. The Bible says this man's **"...delight is in the law of the Lord, and in His law he meditates** [ponders and orally recites] **day and night."**

Actually, Psalm 1:1 provides more insight into what causes spiritual confusion to enter our lives. Let's look at it:

Blessed [happy and hilarious] **is the man who walks not in the counsel of the ungodly, nor stands in the path of sinners, nor sits in the seat of the scornful.**

Notice the progression. The man who doesn't heed the Word of God first walks in the counsel of the ungodly. Then he begins to stand around with the sinner. Finally, he sits down with the people who scorn the things of God.

This could be a picture of many of us at one time or another in our lives. We pray the prayer of faith, truthfully believing God's Word with our whole being that the answer is on its way. But time passes, and nothing happens. All of a sudden, we find ourselves talking about the situation to other Christians who don't believe the Word the way we do. We walk with these Christians, letting them persuade us to think the way they think. Soon doubt and unbelief begins to slip in.

Once we leave our foundation of the Word in favor of what others say, it isn't hard to start standing around with unbelievers, talking to them about our situation. And if we're not careful, the next step will be sitting down with those who scorn and mock the things of God we once held so near and dear to our hearts. Faith in God's Word didn't seem to work for us that one time, so now we are in danger of throwing it all out the window as we begin to mock and scorn the things of God.

I'm telling you, listening to *any* voice that speaks contrary to God's Word is something you want to avoid like the plague. It only breeds confusion and causes you to set your affection on that which will eventually destroy your life.

'Let This Mind Be in You...'

Philippians 3:15 (*KJV*) is a scripture that tells us the positive side of *phroneo* — specifically, what we *should* be setting our affections on:

Let us therefore, as many as be perfect [complete]**, be thus minded: and if in any thing ye be otherwise minded, God shall reveal even this unto you.**

When Paul says we are to be "thus minded" (*phroneo*), he is saying in effect, "Let your affections and your desires go in this direction — press toward the mark for the prize of the high calling of God, which is in union with Christ Jesus." Your affections are to be set on what Jesus has done for you, *not* on the things this world has to offer.

Now let's go back one chapter to Philippians 2:5, which says, **"Let this mind [phroneo] be in you which was also in Christ Jesus."** Paul is saying,

"Let your affections go in this direction. Entertain these thoughts. Let this sentiment be in you that was also in Christ Jesus."

What was that "mind" or *phroneo* that was in Christ Jesus? Verses 6-8 tell us:

Who [Jesus], being in the form of God, did not consider it robbery to be equal with God,
but made Himself of no reputation, taking the form of a bondservant, and coming in the likeness of men.
And being found in appearance as a man, He humbled Himself and became obedient to the point of death, even the death of the cross.

Let's break down these verses to see what is inside them. First, in verse 5, Paul is talking about our common, everyday life when he says, **"Let this mind be in you which was also in Christ Jesus."** We are to let this affection or this sentiment that was also in Christ Jesus be within us all the time in our everyday life — not just when we meet our Christian friends on the street.

What was the "mind" that was in Jesus? **"Who, being in the form of God, did not consider it robbery to be equal with God"** (v. 6). Jesus didn't use His equality with God as a means to get His way in this world or for His own advantage. He recognized His equality with God but never took that equality for granted, always showing reverence to the Father. He never thought His equality with God was His lucky ticket to make it big in this world.

Instead, Jesus **"...made Himself of no reputation, taking the form of a bondservant, and coming in the likeness of men."** That phrase "made Himself of no reputation" means Jesus *emptied* Himself of any display of His deity for personal gain. He didn't make Himself out to be any better than anyone else.

In the same way, you and I are not to use our sonship for personal gain or to get a "free ride" in this world. You see, God's Word always brings us back to sobriety. It never says, "Listen, the Gospel is your free ticket in life." The Word leads us to receive our ambassadorship to be colaborers together with Jesus, not to strut around with the attitude, "Jesus died just for me. I'm a King's kid!"

I find that most people who talk about being a King's kid don't act like children of a king. They act more like King's *spoiled brats* than King's kids! They walk around talking more about what their Father is going to give them than what they can do to dispense God's benefits to others.

I'm not saying we shouldn't believe God for material things for ourselves. God wants every one of us to be rich beyond our wildest expectations and beyond what any bank could ever hold. But He also desires that we follow His ways in order to come to that place of abundance.

Never let your mindset in this life be to take advantage of the inheritance your Father has so sweetly bestowed upon you. You are not merely to gather unto yourself what this world has to offer. Rather, you are to use what God places into your hands to further the Kingdom of God. As you do, God promises that everything you need will be added unto you (Matt. 6:33).

We do not need to use every bit of our minds and our energy to seek after the things of this world. Instead, we are to have the same mind or attitude that Jesus had.

Jesus didn't think His deity made Him any better than any other man walking the face of the earth. He didn't come here and say, "Father, I'm going to use My deity to call down twelve legions of angels so they can get Me out of this mess." Instead, Jesus willingly went through the agony of the Cross because He had set His affections wholly on the one thing that mattered — the Father's will. Jesus had come to this earth to set mankind free, and He was determined to fulfill that divine purpose.

That is the "mind" God wants you to have within you. He is asking you to focus your affections and your desires toward His purposes for your life. Then press toward the mark for the prize of the high calling of God in Christ Jesus!

Establishing a New Way To Think

You now know the scriptural meanings for the four New Testament words for "mind." That foundation is essential if you are going to get rid of confusion in your life and concentrate on renovating your mind.

Now here's another question I want you to ponder: How do we get rid of those sins that seem to hang on long after we get born again? That's a question many of us are confused about. We pray; we cry; we beg God to take those sins away from us. Yet again and again, we stumble in those same areas and end up feeling guilty and condemned. What keeps us in bondage to these sins? Wasn't Jesus supposed to set us free?

If this struggle sounds very familiar to you, it is important for you to realize this: *The problem lies in what you are allowing yourself to listen to in your mind.* You see, you cannot get rid of a sin problem by begging or pleading or crying or struggling in prayer in the middle of the night. You can only get rid of a problem the same way that problem came to you. In this case, that means establishing a new set of thought patterns — only this time you do it according to God's Word.

I want to refer back to my own life as an example. I think it will help you understand what I'm talking about.

I remember the day as a young man when some very negative, perverse things entered my life. Before that day, I had resisted even the thought of doing those things. As long as I did that, the sin couldn't overtake me.

You see, a problem cannot overtake you until you believe it. The moment you believe it is the moment it begins to take charge of your life.

Before that day, something kept telling me in my mind, *This is what you want to do. This is what you want to do. This is what you want to do. This is what you want to do. This is what you want to do.* Although I wasn't a Christian at the time, I instinctively contested that voice in my mind. I repeatedly said to myself, *No, that is NOT what I want to do!*

A person usually won't do something wrong until he first finds someone to agree with him that it's okay, whether he reads it in a magazine or book or talks to someone he looks up to. At that point, his mind will try to justify it, thinking, *Well, everyone else does it. And since all things are lawful for me, it's okay if I do this.* Then he will begin to act on those thoughts. And as he actually commits the sin he has been thinking about, that sin begins to gain power in his life. As Romans 6:16 says, a person becomes a servant to whom he obeys.

So this voice in my mind kept telling me, *This is the way you are. This is what you want to do. This is what you want to do.* The mental struggle was so great that I would have to work out intensely until I was absolutely exhausted just so I could get to sleep. I would run and run and run and run, trying in vain to get away from myself.

I was making the same mistake a lot of people make. Often people even move to another location to get away from their problems — only to find out that their problems move with them!

Whatever problem you run from in life will eventually have to be faced. And if you don't deal with it now, it will only be worse when you are finally forced to deal with it. You may move to another location in order to make a fresh start, and that might work for a while. But as soon as you catch up with yourself, the situation that made you run will be even more difficult to face than it was before.

Therefore, the best thing you can do is deal with the problem now — not next week, not next month, not next year, and not when you get around to it. No matter how bad a situation looks right now, you are better off coming to terms with it today than you will be tomorrow. In fact, the best time to deal with any problem in your life is the first time you see it.

But I didn't understand that back then as an unsaved young man. So I kept running as this voice kept telling me, *This is what you want to do. This is what you want to do. This is what you want to do.*

No, no, no, no, no, no, no, no! I would protest.

Yes, this is what you want to do, would come the reply.

Then the enemy started talking to me in my own voice, saying, *You know, I want to do this. I want to do it!* It was no longer obvious that someone was pushing me from the outside. Now it seemed to be coming from the inside — *I* seemed to be doing the talking in my mind!

The thoughts kept coming: *Hey, I think this is okay. I think this is what I want to do. I'm going to do this!* Meanwhile, I was totally confused. I listened to the contradicting thoughts running through my mind and thought, *Will the real Robb Thompson please stand up?* It was wild!

I would cry and pace the floor in the middle of the night, asking myself, *Oh, God, why can't I just have a normal life? Why do I have so many voices in my mind? Why can't I stop feeling guilty about everything? Why can't I seem to get this right? Why? Why? Why? Why? Why?* Meanwhile, my life was going down, down, down as I started believing that those thoughts came from me.

Not long after that, I got born again in that mental institution. But here's the part that really confused me: After I had a dramatic salvation experience with the Lord, my problems didn't stop! I had no idea at the time that I still had to renew my mind with the Word of God in order to walk free from the devil's mental torment.

The reason my salvation was so dramatic for me was that I had previously been demon-possessed. So when I got born again, all the demons had to leave, which made me tremendously relieved to say the least! But after the newness of being a believer wore off in my life, those old thoughts that used to torment me tried to come back. Every day I'd set out to act like a believer, and every day I'd become convinced that I wanted to do the wrong things I used to do.

You see, the devil tries to talk to you all day long every day of the year. If you let him, he'll talk and talk and talk and talk and talk. That's why you can't afford to let up on the Word of God for even one day. As soon as you do, the enemy will find a way to worm his way back into your mind to deceive and defeat you.

Beating the Devil at His Own Game

How do you combat the devil's condemning, destructive thoughts and establish a new way of thinking? First, you do it with your knowledge that you are the righteousness of God. Second, you do it with Mark 11:24:

"Therefore I say to you, whatever things you ask when you pray, believe that you receive them, and you will have them."

Keep that scripture before your eyes all the time, saying, "I receive by faith all that God says is mine. Therefore, I believe I receive every time I pray!"

There have been times when I've had to walk down the street thinking over and over, *I believe I received it. I believe I received it. I believe I received it. I believe I received it. I believe I received it.* Meditating continually on the Word was the only way I could get that voice in my mind to stop talking to me!

Understand this: God never says to you, "Listen, I know I told you to ask in the Name of Jesus, and I know I said all prayers prayed in Jesus' Name are already answered — but in your case, it's not true." Of course, that's what the devil will tell you. He'll say, "Well, the Bible is true for everyone except you."

Do you want to know what I told the devil when he said that to me? I said, "Listen, I don't really care. Even if what you're telling me is really the truth, devil, I'm going to get what I prayed for anyway, and then I'm going to give it away!" After that, I didn't have much problem with the devil anymore!

You don't ever have to move an inch when the devil tries to talk to you. All he is doing is bluffing. He's checking to see what you will put up with and what you really believe. Now, if you believe that you need to fight him, you'll end up fighting him. But that isn't a good idea because he's stronger than you are.

Get this truth strong in your heart: You don't ever have to put up with the devil's thoughts in your mind. If you won't believe what he says, he can't beat you. *Whatever you don't allow the devil to do, he cannot do.*

I remember the day this truth became real to my own heart. At the time, I was delivering parcels for that parcel delivery company, and the Word was still new to me.

That day I was on a delivery near the Brookfield zoo, and a series of bad thoughts were pounding my mind. Over and over, I heard the same thing: *You want to think these thoughts. You want to think these thoughts. You want to think these thoughts.* I was trying to resist the thoughts, but they were getting stronger, trying to paint sinful pictures inside my mind.

Suddenly this revelation hit my heart: *If these wrong thoughts are not me, I don't need to be ashamed before the Lord about them!*

So I said, "Okay, negative thought, you come with me right now! You are going to tell Jesus what you just told me. I said, *come on!*"

All of a sudden, those thoughts were gone! I thought, *Wait a second, this is getting interesting!* For the first time, I wasn't thinking, *I'm such a bad guy. There's something wrong with me. Jesus is about to jump my case because I'm not as good as I'm supposed to be.*

The next time wrong thoughts began to pound on my mind, I tried it again. "Okay, bad thoughts, you come with me and tell Jesus what you just told me."

Then as we stood before Jesus, I just smiled and told the Lord, "Jesus, You know I love You." Meanwhile, this absolutely putrid, maggoty, good-for-nothing thought was trying to control my mind!

But I just kept standing there in front of Jesus, smiling and telling Him, "Oh, Jesus, I love You. But, Lord, this ugly thought is trying to come between us. He's trying to get me to go with him and leave You. Okay, now, thought, you tell Jesus what you just told me! I mean, if you don't tell Him, I will!"

All of a sudden, the bad thoughts left! And from that day on, my mind started straightening up. Scriptures like Second Corinthians 5:21 had a whole new meaning for me: **"For He made Him who knew no sin to be sin for us, that we might become the righteousness of God in Him."** I finally realized, *Hey, that's talking about me!*

After that, when wrong thoughts tried to take over my mind, they would run smack dab into all the Word residing there and say, "Ah, forget it!"

I'd reply, "It's a good thing you're going, you putrid thought! Otherwise, I'd take you with me to see Jesus so you could tell Him what you're telling me! Just stay away and don't bother me anymore!"

You can do the same thing. Suppose you're walking through life, going along your merry way, when a wrong thought enters your mind: *You know you want to do what you used to do.* Just say, "Okay, thought, you come along with me to see Jesus. Now, tell Jesus what you just told me. Go ahead, tell Him." You'll be amazed at how fast that bad thought leaves!

The next day when more negative thoughts bombard your mind, don't go to your pastor and complain, "I'm just tormented in my mind, Pastor. What am I going to do?" Think about it — why should you be tormented in your mind? That's not the devil's mind — it's *your* mind. You don't need to let him in there if you don't want to.

Just do what you did before. Say, "Come with me, every one of you ungodly thoughts. We're going to go see Jesus together. Now, you tell Him what you told me. Go ahead — tell Him! You don't have the guts to say it again, do you? Well, then, get out of here!" When you turn around, the bad thoughts will be gone!

But rest assured — the devil will try again. You see, all he wants to do is get you to a place where you'll no longer say, "Come with me to see Jesus." He wants you to start thinking again that the problem is you — that *you* are the one who thinks these bad thoughts.

When you believe you're the problem, the devil has a easy time beating up on your mind. You don't want to go to Jesus when you're the problem.

That's why it's important to stay in a neutral position regarding how you think about yourself. Don't think good things about yourself, and don't think bad things about yourself. Just think "*God* things" about yourself!

I don't see myself as good, and I don't see myself as bad. I see myself the way God sees me. That way I don't walk around with guilty feelings, nor do I walk around thinking I'm a great guy. I just know that God loves me and that whatever comes into my life is going to be a blessing.

Even if something negative comes in my life, I know God will do whatever He needs to do to turn that negative thing around and make it into a positive. Why? Because He loves me.

You see, living the Christian life isn't tough; it's really quite simple. The one thing you have to do is believe in the grace of God. When you truly believe in God's grace, you think and speak about yourself only the way God thinks about you. This is so paramount to winning in life.

The devil doesn't want you to know that, so he starts talking to you, talking to you, and talking to you. If he can get you to start listening to him, he'll keep pouring all his poisonous thoughts into your ear until he gains control of your body. At that point, you will do whatever he tells you to do.

You know, there is one thing about the devil — he's not real strong, but he's real consistent. Day in and day out, he keeps speaking to you. And every time he speaks to your mind and you listen, he knows he's gaining a little more ground in your thought life. All he wants to do is control your mind. He knows that whatever controls your mind controls your life. So he comes with his arsenal of negative thoughts, such as:

- *You're sick.*

- *You're poor.*

- *You want to quit your job.*

- *You want somebody else besides your spouse.*

- *Your spouse wants somebody besides you!*

- *You can't relate to people worth a lick.*

But whenever the devil bombards your mind with his ungodly thoughts, just respond to every thought that is contrary to God's Word by saying, *"I'm not buying it, devil!"* Then drive out those wrong thoughts by confessing God's promises in faith.

You may ask, "Well, how much do I need to confess the Word? I already said two verses today." You meditate on and speak the Word until the devil goes away! Until he leaves you alone for good — and that won't happen until you go home to be with Jesus — just keep meditating on and confessing the Word of God. And realize this: Depending on how far your mind sunk into depravity before you knew Jesus, that's how far into "Word-bound thinking" you have to go to acquire "saved brains"!

Confessing What God Says Is True

As I said earlier, whichever voice you listen to in your mind is the one that will win out. That's why it is so important to you as a believer to meditate on and confess God's Word. Nothing is more important in eliminating confusion from your life.

Recently someone told me that he had been diagnosed with chronic fatigue syndrome. I said, "So you feel tired all the time."

"Yes, I'm really weak," this person said.

"Well, there is something for you in the Word of God," I replied. "Joel 3:10 says, 'Let the weak say I am a strong warrior.' Now, notice God did *not* say, 'You who are strong, go around saying you're strong!' It is the weak who are supposed to say — *not* just think — 'I am a strong warrior!'"

Why are the weak supposed to say that? So they can be frustrated? So the knowledge that they are not strong can eat them alive? No! They are to speak those words so their faith can come alive and bring God's strength on the scene to change the situation!

Then this person said to me, "You know, even if I had been saying I was a strong warrior all this time, I don't believe it would have helped me at all."

This person had faith all right, but it was faith in the *disease*, not in *the Word of God*. His attitude was "Listen, can you pray a prayer over me? Can you pray some kind of 'hocus pocus' prayer and make this condition go away? I want my healing, but I want it to come easy!"

But there is no "hocus pocus" way to receive God's promises. As long as you live on this earth, you will face an enemy who wants to steal what is rightfully yours and lead you into defeat. Therefore, in order to win the good fight of faith and enjoy God's blessings in this life, you must make a habit of meditating on and confessing the Word.

Romans 5:2,3 (*KJV*) lets us know that the Christian walk is not always easy:

By whom [Jesus] also we have access by faith into this grace wherein we stand, and rejoice in hope of the glory of God.

And not only so, but we glory in tribulations also: knowing that tribulation [or the trying of our faith] **worketh patience.**

The word "worketh" here is the Greek word *katergazomai*, meaning *to work fully; to finish; to accomplish.*[15] In this context, this word could mean the trying of your faith *will bring patience to the forefront.*

Verse 3 (*NAS*) then says that patience produces *proven character.* Therefore, patience — or consistency in the Word of God during adversity or challenge — will produce godly character. It also produces a renovated mind!

So as you work on renewing your mind day by day, keep Second Corinthians 4:17 in mind:

For our light affliction, which is but for a moment, is working for us a far more exceeding and eternal weight of glory.

Your central focus should always be that "exceeding and eternal weight of glory" up ahead of you. When you go home to be with the Lord, there will be no cancer, no marital problems, no disobedient children, no poverty. You won't have to pay the utilities or the mortgage company. You're going to a place that's filled with joy, peace, and happiness.

Take your focus off the trials and challenges you face in this life. There is an exceeding and eternal weight of glory awaiting you that makes all your earthly affliction seem light in comparison! When

---

[15] Strong, p. 41, #2716.

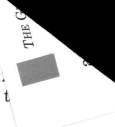

your focus is on the joy set before you in
"cross" you might have to bear (Heb. 12:
able to overcome any type of pressure t
your way!

The Profession of Our Faith:
Our Heavenly Calling

You know, the Church doesn't talk much about
what we have waiting for us in Heaven. Yet God's
Word tells us that life on this earth is worthwhile
because we have Heaven and an eternity with the
Father to look forward to. That's why we are not to
look at the things of this world.

Along that line, Hebrews 3:1 (*KJV*) calls us
**"...holy brethren, partakers of the heavenly
calling...."** The word "partakers" means *one who is
a partner.*[16] We are partners with God in the heavenly calling — the calling God has given us *from*
Heaven to point us *toward* Heaven.

Verse 1 (*KJV*) goes on to say, **"...consider the
Apostle and High Priest of our profession,
Christ Jesus."** One meaning of the word "consider"
in this context is *to put down upon.*[17] We are to "put
our minds down upon" and consider closely our confession of the Lord Jesus Christ. We are to think
about and direct our minds to the Apostle, the One
whom God has commissioned as High Priest to go
before God on behalf of our profession of faith. In a
sense, we are to "hold down" our confession of faith
in Jesus and never allow it to fly away from us. And

---

[16] W. E. Vine, *An Expository Dictionary of New Testament Words* (Old
Tappan, New Jersey: Fleming H. Revell Co., 1966), p. 161.
[17] Reinecker and Rogers, p. 671.

as we hold fast to our confession of faith, we will be changed by it.

The word "profession" can be interchanged by two other words: "confession" and "agreement." Jesus is the Apostle and High Priest of our agreement with God. We agree with what God says, and Jesus takes our confession of faith and presents it in the high court of Heaven on our behalf.

But remember — the words of your mouth are actually your thoughts expressed. You have to continually *think* God's thoughts before you will be able to continually *speak* God's words. Therefore, the first step to victory is a conquered, renovated mind — clear of all confusion and focused on things above, not on the things of this earth!

8

SCRIPTURAL STRATEGIES FOR CONQUERING THE MIND

The outcome of your life will be determined by who and what controls your mind. That is an awesome thought to consider. It demonstrates how important it is to learn God's strategies for conquering your carnal mind and subjecting to it to His Word until it is unmoved and unaffected by the world's thinking.

I want to show you some of these scriptural strategies for conquering the mind, focusing on scriptures that center around one word: *let*. We're going to talk about what we *should* let and what we should *not* let happen in our lives on the road to renovating our minds.

Let God Be True

First, in Romans 3:4 we find the most basic strategy for conquering the mind: **"...Let God be true but every man a liar...."** Paul is saying, "Let God be found to be true even though every man is found to be a liar." You see, unless a man is saying what God is saying, that man is a liar. A liar is not a person who goes around telling untruths all the time. A liar is a person who continually speaks wrongly about God's Word.

"Let God to be found to be true, though every man is found to be a liar." This emphasizes the continual state of rightness regarding that which is written. The Word of God is the truth in every situation you could ever face, even if you never believe it. The Word of God is the truth, whether or not you ever want to line up your mind to it. God's Word never changes.

You're the righteousness of God whether you ever believe it or not. You are free from your past, whether you ever believe it or not. You are a new creature, whether you ever believe it or not. You are healthy, whether you ever believe it or not. You are prosperous, whether you ever believe it or not. You are free from guilt, whether you ever experience it or not.

Have you ever seen a young tree with a stake pounded in the ground next to it to help it grow straight and strong? Without the stake to guide its growth, that little tree would grow wild.

Your life in Christ is the same way. It will grow wild unless you depend on God's Word to guide you. You may have God's life in you; you may know the Word of God is true. But you have to make God's Word your "stake" to keep your life straight and true. Otherwise, you will grow wild, and you will never come to a place of maturity.

Do you want to be one of those tall, straight trees **"...planted by the rivers of water, that brings forth its fruit in its season, whose leaf also shall not wither..."** (Ps. 1:3)? Then let God be true even if every voice in this world is found to be a liar. Refuse to allow any thoughts to reside in your mind that contradict God's Word. With the Word as your absolute guide to truth, you can conquer your carnal mind whether it wants to be conquered or not!

Let the Peace of God Rule!

Colossians 3:15 gives us another scriptural strategy for conquering the mind:

> **And let the peace of God rule in your hearts, to which also you were called in one body; and be thankful.**

"Let the peace of God rule." That word "rule" is an interesting term. It essentially means *to referee or to be an umpire who calls a decision and decides between.*[18] Let the peace of God be an umpire within your heart, helping you decide which way to go. When you have to make decisions between two opinions, let God's peace make that distinction. Allow

---

[18] Ibid., p. 307.

that peace to rule in you. When you don't know what to do, follow peace.

Verse 16 gives us something else we should let happen as we work on renovating our minds:

Let the word of Christ dwell in you richly in all wisdom, teaching and admonishing one another in psalms and hymns and spiritual songs, singing with grace in your hearts to the Lord.

You are to allow the Word of Christ to dwell in you — to take up residence in you and to make its home in you. Peace will be the umpire in the heart where God's Word has made its home.

Now, it's interesting to me that the Bible tells us to *let* peace and *let* the Word of Christ do something in our lives. How could we let these two spiritual forces do something if they weren't already present in our lives?

The reason I can let peace rule is that it is already in my heart. A storm may be brewing all around the peace of Christ that resides within me. But as long as I allow that peace to be my umpire, the one called to decide between two points of contention, I will make it through that storm unharmed and victorious!

Let No Corrupt Communication Come Out of Your Mouth

Now let's talk about what we are to *let not* happen in our lives as we seek to acquire "saved brains." Ephesians 4:29 (*KJV*) says this:

Let no corrupt communication proceed out of your mouth, but that which is good to the use of edifying, that it may minister grace unto the hearers.

Let's break this verse down a little bit. As I mentioned earlier, the word "corrupt" refers to something that is *rank, foul, putrid, horrible, and disgusting.*[19] So Paul is saying, "Let no rank, foul, putrid, rotten, worthless, and disgusting speech proceed or come out of your mouth. Speak only words that are *edifying.*"

The word "edifying" just means that your words are to build up people who hear them rather than tear them down. Paul goes on to say that your words are to minister *grace* to the hearer. In other words, you are to speak words that bring benefit, pleasure, and profit to the hearer.

Why is it so important that you let not corrupt communication proceed out of your mouth? *Because you can never get control of your mind and you can never continually think right thoughts unless you learn to speak right words.*

So every time you enter a conversation with a person, let it always be said that you ministered grace, brought benefit, and even gave pleasure to the person who heard what you were saying. When the other person walks away from a conversation with you, let him say, "That was good! Man, that did something for me. I just want talk to that person

---

[19] Reinecker and Rogers, p. 534.

again because I know he [or she] is going to say something good!"

Proverbs 18:21 says, **"Death and life are in the power of the tongue, and those who love it will eat its fruit."** So speak life, and enjoy the fruit of those life-giving words in every aspect of your life!

'Let Us Not Grow Weary in Doing Good'

Galatians 6:9 presents a very important strategy when it comes to conquering the mind:

And let us not grow weary while doing good, for in due season we shall reap if we do not lose heart.

I like the way this verse reads in the *Phillips* translation:

Let us not grow tired of doing good, for, unless we throw in our hand, the ultimate harvest is assured.[20]

The phrase "let us not grow weary" tells you that you are not to give in to evil or to lose heart and become a coward. For instance, have you ever given in to something that was wrong because you got tired of fighting it? That is in part what Paul is talking about. And that can easily happen when you're in the process of taking control of your mind. At times you'll have to fight from growing weary and giving in to the devil's bombardment of wrong thoughts.

---

[20] J. B. Phillips, *The New Testament in Modern English* (New York: MacMillan Co., 1958), p. 409.

Paul goes on to say, **"And let us not grow weary while doing good...."** In other words, you are not to grow weary in doing what is right and in making sure your thoughts and actions correspond to who you are in Christ Jesus.

Why are you not to grow weary in well doing? **"...For in due season we shall reap...."** There *will* be a harvest of that for which you have believed. There will be a harvest for all the hours you have meditated on the Word and the words of faith you have spoken day by day. Unless you grow weary and "throw in your hand," the ultimate harvest is assured!

So don't give in to evil. Don't lose heart. Don't get tired and let go of your hope. Don't let yourself grow weary on your way to conquering your mind!

Let Not Sin Reign

Romans 6:12 (*KJV*) tells us something else we are to "let not" in order to take control of our minds:

Let not sin therefore reign in your mortal body, that ye should obey it in the lusts thereof.

The word "reign" means *to rule as king*.[21] Do not allow sin to rule as king until you feel compelled to obey the driving pressures that come against you. Do not allow yourself to be driven by anything that is outside the boundaries of God's Word. Paul warns, "Let it not be!"

---

[21] Reinecker and Rogers, p. 362.

Then Paul goes on to say in verse 13 (*KJV*):

Neither yield ye your members as instruments of unrighteousness unto sin: but yield yourselves unto God, as those that are alive from the dead, and your members as instruments of righteousness unto God.

The word "yield" essentially means *to present* or *to place beside*. In this context, it can also mean *to put oneself at sin's disposal.*[22] What are you not to yield? Paul gives the answer: **"...your members as instruments of unrighteousness unto sin...."** This word "instruments" refers to *tools or weapons of war.*[23]

Paul is saying, "Don't allow your sin to become 'king' in your life, ruling over you and causing you to obey its driving pressures. And do not yield your body as a tool or a weapon of unrighteousness, resulting in wrong actions. Instead, yield your members as tools or weapons of righteousness unto God, as one who is alive from the dead."

So the key question is this: Will you let sin reign as ruler in your life? The answer to that question depends on whether or not you believe the Word of God, because all sin finds its root in unbelief. When you don't believe God's Word, sin reigns as king in your life, compelling you to yield the members of your body as instruments — weapons or tools — of unrighteousness.

---

[22] Ibid.
[23] Ibid.

How do you yield your members? The first "member" you yield is your mind. When a thought comes to your mind, your mind either rejects that thought or allows it to germinate. Thoughts that you dwell on and allow to remain, whether good or bad, will eventually become words or actions.

Thus, your thoughts determine whether you yield your members as instruments of righteousness or instruments of unrighteousness unto death. Sinful actions are not just the result of bad habits; they are the result of bad *thoughts*.

Line Upon Line, Precept Upon Precept

Let's go through the process in more detail. We know that God builds a foundation of truth into our lives line upon line, precept upon precept, here a little, there a little (Isa. 28:10). Well, the devil takes away the same way God builds — line upon line, precept upon precept, here a little, there a little.

First, it starts with a thought: *You don't need to be as committed to God as other people tell you. You can compromise. It's all right.*

You dwell on that thought for a while. Then another thought comes: *Come on, you can have church at home. What's the big deal? You can get as much out of listening to that preacher on television as you do your own pastor!*

You entertain that thought as well. Another wrong thought comes, then another. Each one finds a receptive audience as you allow these thoughts to take up residence in your mind.

Soon you notice a difference in your Christian walk. All of a sudden when you pray for people, you don't feel God's anointing anymore. When you lay hands on people, you don't feel God's power shoot out from you the way you used to. When you speak God's Word, it doesn't come out like fire anymore; it just sounds like any other words. You see, Satan has taken away the same way God gave.

Now, the enemy can't take away the knowledge you have in your mind. But he *can* take away the deep-seated anointing that comes forth from the knowledge of God. Satan takes away that anointing line upon line, precept upon precept, a little bit of compromise here, and a little bit of backing off there.

I see it all the time. People start thinking, *I know we've been believing and standing on the Word for a long time, but now I think we need to go on a little vacation. We deserve a break from this fight of faith!*

Here's how it happens in the local church: Some people get very excited when they first hear God's Word preached with power. I'm telling you, they're turned on to the Word of God! You can't stop them! They're the first ones at every church service and the last ones to leave. They come up to me and say, "God's Word is so alive to me, Pastor — I just don't know what to do! I can't even sleep at night because God's Word is so alive!"

Because these people are committed to the Word of God, God begins to exalt them by giving them a position in His local body. But with the promotion comes added responsibility. Little by little, these people become so involved in the church that they stop spending as much time in God's Word as they once did. They start thinking that they're too busy, that they need more time to just relax. But it isn't a hunger for more time in the Word that makes them think that way. They just want some extra time to watch a little television and have fun.

Soon these people's zeal for the Word dampens, their anointing weakens, and they don't even know what has happened to them. But I'll tell you what happened — they have traded their *walk with* God for their *work for* God!

Tear Down Every Mental Stronghold

So it all begins with a thought that you dwell on, followed by another and another. These thoughts then begin to paint inner pictures, which later become *strongholds.*

Second Corinthians 10:4,5 talks about these mental strongholds:

> **For the weapons of our warfare are not carnal but mighty in God for pulling down strongholds,**
> **casting down arguments and every high thing that exalts itself against the knowledge of God, bringing every thought into captivity to the obedience of Christ.**

God is the One who infuses you with power so you can effectively use your spiritual weapons to pull down every stronghold in your mind.

Notice that phrase **"...bringing every thought into captivity to the obedience of Christ."** You are to "arrest" every thought that doesn't coincide with God's Word and take it as prisoner, treating it as an abominable, devilish criminal that has come to steal from you. When you *don't* do that, the wrong thought eventually becomes an imagination.

Now, the word "imagination" is really just a series of pictures in your mind. These pictures can begin to take up most of your waking hours. And if you don't deal with your carnal imagination — if those inner pictures go unchecked — they develop into strongholds in your mind.

Most Christians live with a tremendous number of strongholds in their lives because they never check their thoughts. Those wrong thoughts form inner pictures; those pictures develop into strongholds; and the strongholds in their minds produce wrong actions. However, if they had dealt with the wrong thoughts in the first place, they would never have had to deal with their sinful actions!

That's what I mean when I say sin isn't committing wrong actions — sin ultimately results from *not believing God's Word*.

So take into captivity every wrong thought to the obedience of Christ. No matter what that thought

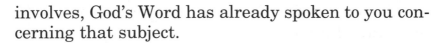

involves, God's Word has already spoken to you concerning that subject.

For instance, if the thought is a temptation to lust, John 15:3 (*KJV*) gives you God's answer:

Now ye are clean [morally pure, sinless, and unstained] **through the word which I have spoken unto you.**

If the thought is a temptation to steal, Ephesians 4:28 tells you what God says about that as well:

Let him who stole steal no longer, but rather let him labor, working with his hands what is good, that he may have something to give him who has need.

Let's say a thought comes to your mind, *My husband doesn't love me.* But you can meditate on Ephesians 5:25, which says your husband loves you as Christ loves the church. Or perhaps you think, *My wife never listens to me!* You can counter that thought with Ephesians 5:24, which says your wife submits, subjects, and adapts herself to you as a service to the Lord.

You see, my wife Linda doesn't subject herself to me as a service to me. She is doing it as unto the Lord, to whom she has committed her life. That's why I want her to deal with God, not with me. I know that as she is pure in heart toward God, I never have to wonder if she will be pure in heart toward me. In the same way, as I seek to obey God, Linda doesn't ever need to wonder about my natural love for her because I'm going to love her as Christ loves the Church.

So no matter what situation arises, my friend, nothing could ever come into your life that is not covered by the Word of God. God's Word covers every single area of your life. And for every thought, imagination, or stronghold that exalts itself against the knowledge of God, there is an divine antidote for it in the Word.

You can be delivered from every stronghold a lot quicker than it took for you to erect it in your mind. How? By believing you're one with God. By believing you're a new creature in Christ. By believing the Word of God is true about you. By staying out of confusion and refusing to go after what this world has to offer!

Keep Your Thoughts in Check

The truth is, conquering our minds is a lot simpler than people have made it out to be. There is only one thing that is difficult about it. You have to be willing to consistently keep your thoughts in check, bringing them into subjection to the Word before the enemy can take advantage of you.

Galatians 6:1 (*KJV*) gives us some insight about how the devil tries to do this:

Brethren, if a man be overtaken in a fault, ye which are spiritual, restore such an one in the spirit of meekness; considering thyself, lest thou also be tempted.

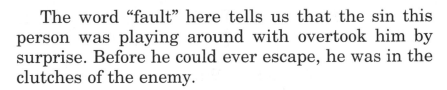

The word "fault" here tells us that the sin this person was playing around with overtook him by surprise. Before he could ever escape, he was in the clutches of the enemy.

Then he said, **"...ye which are spiritual, restore...."** The word "restore" is the same word used for the setting of a broken bone. Those called to restore are the "spiritual" ones in the Body of Christ — those who believe the Word of God and are not being tripped up in their minds by the devil's devices. These are the believers who must reset the "broken bones" of their brothers and sisters who have been tricked into not believing the Word of God and are now being held captive by the enemy.

My friend, you are engaged in a war — a battle for what is between your ears. What are you going to believe? For instance, it's easy to heal the sick. It's easy to cast out devils. I mean, there is no magic to it whatsoever. God's Word said it, so it's just a breeze!

But the challenge comes when you lay your hands on the person and have to stay fully persuaded that what God has promised, He will also perform. You *can't just lay your hands on the sick and then see what God will do.* God isn't going to do anything in that case, because you're not believing that He will!

So don't let the enemy take advantage of you in your mind. Keep your thoughts in check, and never let up on your guard. It's a battle, and that means there is an opportunity to lose as you seek to conquer your mind. But if you will stay in the good fight of faith and refuse to give up, you *will* win!

You Are a Winner — So Hold On to Your Victory!

How do I know you'll win? Because if you are skilled in the Word of righteousness, you are someone who understands that you start out in the fight of faith as a winner. You don't have to strive to be a winner. You are not a loser trying to win. You are a winner when you start, and someone is trying to steal your victory.

For instance, when sickness shows up, you aren't a sick person trying to get healed. Rather; you are a healthy person, and someone is just trying to steal your health.

Hebrews 5:12-14 talks about those who are *unskilled* in the Word of righteousness:

For though by this time you ought to be teachers, you need someone to teach you again the first principles of the oracles of God; and you have come to need milk and not solid food.

For everyone who partakes only of milk is unskilled in the word of righteousness, for he is a babe.

But solid food belongs to those who are of full age, that is, those who by reason of use have their senses exercised to discern both good and evil.

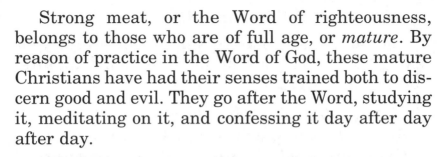

Strong meat, or the Word of righteousness, belongs to those who are of full age, or *mature*. By reason of practice in the Word of God, these mature Christians have had their senses trained both to discern good and evil. They go after the Word, studying it, meditating on it, and confessing it day after day after day.

To become one of those mature believers, you must train your senses according to the Word until they are keen and sharp. Then when Satan tries to trick you in your mind, you won't fall for it. Your senses will tell you that those thoughts are not right. You'll be trained to discern what is right and what is wrong, and that in turn will help you keep the victory that is already yours.

You know, every day each and every one of us go through a battle over who controls our minds. You may say, "I'm not in a battle right now." But you *are* in a battle, whether you know it or not. And if you're not actively fighting the good fight of faith, you are probably allowing Satan's kingdom to run right over you!

Of course, if that's what you desire, you can have it. If you want to lose in life, that's your prerogative. If you want to live a mediocre Christian life, you can have that too. But it's my job to tell you that you don't have to settle for that. You can *win* in life, and it all starts with not letting sin reign in your life!

Let Us Examine Ourselves

Let's look at one more very important strategy for taking control of your mind. It is found in First Corinthians 11:27,28:

Therefore whoever eats this bread or drinks this cup of the Lord in an unworthy manner will be guilty of the body and blood of the Lord.
But LET A MAN EXAMINE HIMSELF, and so let him eat of the bread and drink of the cup.

This scripture is referring to the subject of Communion, but the principle of examining ourselves is relevant to every realm of life, especially the realm of the mind.

Now, the important thing about Communion is not whether wine or grape juice is used. The purpose of Communion is not found in the bread and the wine, but in what these elements represent — the broken body and the shed blood of Jesus Christ, the Son of God.

In the context of this passage of Scripture, the bread and the wine are not the focus of discussion. Rather, the focus is on how the believers at the church of Corinth were treating one another. They were not correctly esteeming each other nor discerning each other's value and worth in the eyes of God.

Why do I say that? Because verses 33 and 34 explain the problem Paul was addressing:

Therefore, my brethren, when you come together to eat, wait for one another. But if anyone is hungry, let him eat at home, lest you come together for judgment. And the rest I will set in order when I come.

When the Corinthian believers gathered to partake of Communion together, some were eating and drinking the elements before the others arrived. They weren't waiting for their fellow believers; therefore, they weren't properly esteeming them.

The sacrament of Communion is supposed to be a time when believers commune together, remembering as they partake of the bread and wine what Jesus has provided for them through His death and resurrection. But the Corinthian believers were selfishly going after the *elements* to satisfy their stomachs rather than *the reason behind the elements* — to enjoy a time of worship and communion with one another in the Presence of the Lord.

That's why Paul said, "Wait for one another when you come together, and if any man is hungry, let him eat at home so you don't put yourself under condemnation."

Verses 30,31 give us further insight into the situation in the Corinthian church:

For this reason many are weak and sick among you, and many sleep.
For if we would judge ourselves, we would not be judged.

What do these verses tell us? These people were judging each other! By eating and drinking the Communion elements before their fellow believers, some of the Corinthian believers were judging the others as not being of value to God. They were no longer including those believers in the covenant they shared with God. And by passing judgment upon their fellow believers, these people were eating and drinking condemnation to themselves, not discerning or understanding the value of the Body of Christ (1 Cor. 11:29).

Judge the Fruit, Not the Person

In light of this situation, let's now consider Paul's instruction to us as believers: **"...let a man examine himself..."** (v. 28). First, let me make this important point: *The Word of God never gives us the right to examine another person.*

You may say, "Well, that's not true because there are scriptures that tell me to examine and to judge."

Yes, but there is something you may not have taken into account. God never gave us the right to judge another person; He only gave us the right and responsibility to judge a person's *fruit*.

Matthew 7:16 says, **"You will know them by their fruits...."** We must be able to look behind a person to see what kind of trail they are leaving behind them. We have to deal with the fruit, but we are never to judge the *person*. God may hate the sin, but He still loves the sinner, so it is up to us to

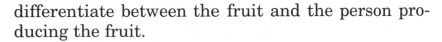

differentiate between the fruit and the person producing the fruit.

Fortunately, it is easy to make that differentiation. You must deal with a person according to his *actions*, but you must love him according to the *Word*. You are to believe the Word about him, but you still have to deal with him according to his actions until his actions line up with the Word of God.

That's why the Word of God tells you that you are to be wise as a serpent and as harmless as a dove (Matt. 10:16). You can't obey that scripture without examining fruit. But always keep this in mind: As you examine the fruit in a person's life, never cross the line by judging the *person*.

Romans 2:1 clearly explains this principle of not judging others:

> **Therefore you are inexcusable, O man, whoever you are who judge, for in whatever you judge another you condemn yourself; for you who judge practice the same things.**

Judgment actually comes into our lives when we pass over areas in our lives that *we* need to change and instead take notice of the need for change in others' lives. If we are making this mistake, we are probably ever ready to believe the worst about another person — but appalled when someone else does the same to us!

So get it straight in your mind once and for all —
God never calls on you to judge another person. As
Romans 14:4 says:

**Who are you to judge another's ser-
vant? To his own master he stands or
falls. Indeed, he will be made to stand, for
God is able to make him stand.**

God will deal with those around you. He just
wants you to examine *yourself*.

At least once a week when I wake up in the morning, God brings something to my attention about
which I need to judge myself. For instance, recently
He reminded me of something I needed to deal with.
I had said something to someone that wasn't wrong;
actually, it was absolutely the truth. But my motive
wasn't exactly what it needed to be, and I knew I
had to judge myself and get it right before God.

You're the only one who can judge your motives.
No one else can do it for you. You see, people can
often be fooled. You probably know how to mask a
wrong motive while holding a conversation with
someone. That's why you have to examine yourself
on a regular basis. You never want to find yourself
sitting in the seat of the scornful.

This scriptural principle is so important for you
to understand as you seek to take control of your
mind. You can never really be free in your own mind
as long as you are focusing on whether or not someone else is doing wrong.

Of course, those who hold a place of eldership within a local body will be called upon to deal with things that are wrong or negative. Church leaders often have to make decisions regarding individuals based on what they believe God's Word says about particular situations.

But whether you are a leader or a layperson in the Church, just be ever ready to believe the best about every person. Then concentrate on examining *yourself*.

The Danger of Critical Words

Have you ever allowed your words to get in a negative, critical vein from which it was very difficult to extract yourself? Matthew 12:37 warns you of the danger of speaking those negative words:

For by your words you will be justified, and by your words you will be condemned.

You are condemning yourself when you use words against someone else. Remember, Romans 2:1 says that if you are judging someone else, you are condemning yourself because you are admitting that you do the very same thing.

Using your mouth to talk about another believer's faults and sins should be considered off limits. You can actually put yourself in danger of physical death if you continually use your mouth against other people. Your critical words give Satan easy access, which he will use to start taking control of your mind.

What that person sitting next to you is doing is of absolutely no consequence to you. And in your homes, what your mate is doing or not doing to obey the Word of God is not your business either. It's his or her responsibility to walk on the Word of God. You can't do it for your spouse, because the entire time you're trying to get him or her to obey God's Word, you're not walking in the Word for yourself. Just stick to the divine admonition in First Corinthians 11:31: **"For if we would judge ourselves, we would not be judged."**

Matthew 7:1 says the same thing in another way: **"Judge not, that you be not judged."** The *Johnson* paraphrase says, **"Do not spend your time deciding whether people are good or bad, and then you won't be afraid that they or God are deciding whether you are good or bad."**[24]

You know, you never need to wonder what someone else is thinking about you if you don't think negative things about others. And if you don't talk about another person in front of others, you don't need to wonder if other people are talking about you.

The *Johnson* paraphrase of Matthew 7:2-5 has a unique way of making Jesus' message very clear:[25]

> **Whatever standard that you use to evaluate other persons, you will use the same standard to evaluate yourself. And with whatever limited knowledge you measure out their punishment, you will measure out your own.**

---

[24] Johnson, p. 28.
[25] Ibid.

In the process of evaluating another person, why do you see a speck in a brother's eye while you are oblivious to the two-by-four in your own?

I must say, it is quite presumptuous for you to offer to wipe a speck out of his eye when you might jab his good eye with the two-by-four in your own!

O, pretender, take the two-by-four out of your eye so that you will not injure your brother when you are wiping the speck out of his. (Maybe when you suffer the pain of removing the two-by-four, you may be willing for your brother to wipe his own eye.)

God help us all as we learn to focus on our own "two-by-fours" and let our brothers and sisters in the Lord take care of their "specks"!

When We Sow Judgment, We *Reap* Judgment

So if we are going to conquer our minds, we must stop thinking and talking negatively about how other people are doing in their spiritual walk. Otherwise, Matthew 7:2 will apply to us, which says in essence, "The amount of judgment and punishment we measure out to someone else is the very same amount God will measure out to us."

Obadiah 15 says something similar: **"...As you have done, it shall be done to you; your reprisal shall return upon your own head."** That which you and I say and do will return unto us once again. If we judge others, we will reap judgment unto ourselves. If we sow seeds of mercy and grace, we will reap the same in our own lives.

Of course, as believers, we shouldn't want to do something right for someone else just so we can have something right happen to us. We are in union with God; therefore, we want to do things the way *He* does them.

I don't avoid judging people just because I don't want to be judged myself. The main reason I don't judge people is the love of God that has been shed abroad in my heart by the Holy Spirit (Rom. 5:5). Also, I don't judge others because God's Word tells me I shouldn't!

If you believe the Word of God concerning who you are in Christ, you will not violate another person by walking out of love. If you believe what the Word says, you won't judge. You won't condemn. You won't walk in unforgiveness.

Nevertheless, you and I cannot escape the law of sowing and reaping operating in our lives. As Genesis 8:22 says, **"While the earth remains, seedtime and harvest, cold and heat, winter and summer, and day and night shall not cease."** Under the natural law of seedtime and harvest that governs this world, we *will* reap whatever we sow in thought, word, and action.

Are You 'In the Faith'?

Let's look at another scripture that commands us to examine ourselves. Second Corinthians 13:5 says,

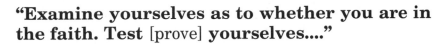

"Examine yourselves as to whether you are in the faith. Test [prove] yourselves...."

Now, this phrase "examine yourselves" just means to be approved and shown to be correct after being scrutinized. That doesn't just mean that you are to examine whether or not you are believing God correctly in any area of your life. It means you must make sure you are acting in a completely well-rounded, balanced way within the family of God.

You must ask yourself, "Is my life in balance according to the whole counsel of God? Am I walking in agreement with God's Word in every area of my life? Am I living in the sphere of 'the faith' — the walk of love, righteousness, health, and prosperity?"

Verse 5 goes on to say, **"...Do you not know yourselves, that Jesus Christ is in you? — unless indeed you are disqualified."** The *King James Version* puts that last phrase this way: **"...except ye be reprobates."**

The word "know" in this verse is not the word *gnosis*, which just refers to general knowledge. It is the Greek word *epiginosko*, a word coined by the apostle Paul to mean *revelation knowledge.*

Paul is saying, "Haven't you received revelation knowledge about this subject yet? Don't you know yourself that Christ Jesus is in you — unless, of course, you are disqualified as a reprobate. I mean, come on, fellows!"

Notice the three words *examine, test,* and *know* in verse 5. First, we examine ourselves. In our personal examination, we *test* ourselves, or we put ourselves on trial. We ask: "Do I reject the counsel of God's Word in any area of my life?"

Finally, we *know* ourselves. In other words, it is supernaturally revealed to us what it means to have Jesus Christ live in us through the Person of the Holy Spirit. Jesus' Presence and His love in our lives provides the bridle we need to keep us from ever moving out of the faith and becoming reprobates.

What Is a 'Reprobate'?

When you understand what it means to be a reprobate, you'll better understand the importance of regularly examining yourself so you never become one.

We have this idea that reprobates are heathen from another country. We say things like, "That wild man from Borneo is sure a reprobate!" Of course, unbelievers can be reprobates. But could believers be reprobates as well? This verse lets us know they can. How do they get that way? They don't examine themselves the way they should and therefore end up walking out of the faith.

Romans 1:28 (*KJV*) talks about people whose rebellious actions resulted in reprobate minds:

And even as they did not like to retain God in their knowledge, God gave them over to a reprobate mind, to do those things which are not convenient.

This verse is speaking about heathen people who **"...although they knew God, they did not glorify Him as God, nor were thankful, but became futile in their thoughts, and their foolish hearts were darkened"** (v. 21). Verses 22-27 then relate all the terrible things these heathen people did because they refused to allow God to remain in their consciousness. At that point, God refused to allow them to stay in *His* consciousness and gave them over to a reprobate mind.

The Greek word for the word "reprobate" is the word *adokimos*. It essentially means *to be thrown away as trash; to be useless and rejected after examination; to be trodden down; good for nothing.*

Thus, a reprobate mind is a mind that is no longer useful to God. It has been so seared by sin and rebellion that it can never be used again (although a reprobate Christian may be able to recover by the grace and mercy of God).

What is it that causes a person to start down the road to becoming a reprobate? James 4:17 has a succinct answer to that question:

> **Therefore, to him who knows to do good and does not do it, to him it is sin.**

So a general definition for a reprobate is a person, whether saved or unsaved, who knows what God has declared to be right and still doesn't do it.

Romans 1:28-32 explains what happens to people who have reprobate minds:

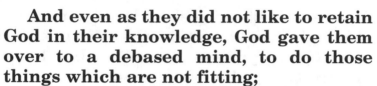

> **And even as they did not like to retain God in their knowledge, God gave them over to a debased mind, to do those things which are not fitting;**
>
> **being filled with all unrighteousness, sexual immorality, wickedness, covetousness, maliciousness; full of envy, murder, strife, deceit, evil-mindedness; they are whisperers,**
>
> **backbiters, haters of God, violent, proud, boasters, inventors of evil things, disobedient to parents,**
>
> **undiscerning, untrustworthy, unloving, unforgiving, unmerciful;**
>
> **who, knowing the righteous judgment of God, that those who practice such things are worthy of death, not only do the same but also approve of those who practice them.**

I don't know about you, but I'm not interested in becoming a reprobate. I don't ever want to become unusable to God!

Strive for the Mastery!

In First Corinthians 9:24-27 (*KJV*), the apostle Paul paints us a picture of a person who will never end up as a reprobate. This passage of Scripture includes the same Greek word *adokimos* that is translated "reprobate" in Second Corinthians 13:5. However, we'll see later that this scripture uses a different English word to describe it.

First, let's look at the entire passage:

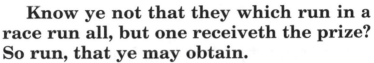

Know ye not that they which run in a race run all, but one receiveth the prize? So run, that ye may obtain.

And every man that striveth for the mastery is temperate in all things. Now they do it to obtain a corruptible crown; but we an incorruptible.

I therefore so run, not as uncertainly; so fight I, not as one that beateth the air:

But I keep under my body, and bring it into subjection: lest that by any means, when I have preached to others, I myself should be a castaway.

When Paul talks about running in a race, he is alluding to a racing arena in the Greek Olympic games that was shaped like a parallelogram and about 200 yards long and 30 yards wide. The "prize" was a crown made out of olive branches, which a person would receive after winning the Olympic race.

Now, let me tell you about the race for just a moment. The Olympian athletes ran this race once a year. Let's suppose the person who won the race one year was named Publius. This man Publius walks over to what was called the Bama, the "reward seat," to receive the crown. As he stands before the Bama, the king places the crown of olive branches upon his head, and the crowd wildly cheers.

But Publius doesn't just receive the crown as a prize; he is also given great fame and popularity. After the race, a runner runs to his hometown to

spread the news. The townspeople then send car-
penters out to knock a large hole in the city wall.
Once that is accomplished, they send a chariot out to
receive their very own celebrity as he returns to his
hometown.

The chariot then rides Publius through that hole
in the wall as he makes his grand entrance. He is
the only person who will ever ride through that hole
in the city walls. Afterwards, the townspeople put a
plaque upon that wall declaring, "PUBLIUS WON
THE RACE!"

Publius is famous from that moment forward. He
will never pay for anything his entire life. He will
never have to pay taxes. All his shopping will be
paid for by tax dollars. Not only that, but his parents
will be taken care of for the rest of their lives as well.

All of us would like to win that race, wouldn't we?
But, you see, the Greeks ran that race to obtain a
corruptible crown. After all, at the end of Publius'
life, it was all over! On the other hand, we as believers run our spiritual race to obtain an *incorruptible*
crown.

Let's look at verse 25 (*KJV*) again: **"And every
man that striveth for the mastery is temperate
in all things...."** What does the phrase "striveth for
the mastery" mean?

Long before the Olympic race was held, a search
was conducted to find the fastest men in the land.
Once a man was chosen to run, he prepared to win
the race months in advance, enduring a rigorous

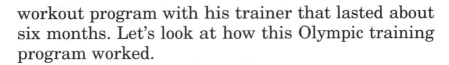

workout program with his trainer that lasted about six months. Let's look at how this Olympic training program worked.

First, the trainer takes the runner out to the parallelogram and says, "I want you to run as fast as you can around this racing track." The runner runs around the track as fast as his legs can carry him as his trainer times him. But when he gets back to his coach, the coach just smiles and says, "Here — put these weights around your ankles and run again."

Run with these weights on my ankles? the runner thinks incredulously.

Nevertheless, the athlete puts on the weights and once again runs his hardest around the track. At the end of his run, he asks his trainer, "How did I do?"

"Not well enough," his trainer replies. "You haven't done well enough until you can run around the track in the very same amount of time that you ran *without* the weights!"

So the athlete runs and runs and runs, striving for the mastery. Finally, he runs around the track with the weights in exactly the same time he ran without the weights. He thinks, *NOW I'll be able to take off these weights!*

But instead, the trainer puts even heavier weights on the runner's ankles and tells him to do the same thing all over again! Once again, the runner has to run again and again and again until he matches the time he ran in the beginning without any weights.

During those six months of intense training, the runner can't have any contact with home. His parents don't know what happened to him. He can't even write to his girlfriend! He doesn't know anything about what is going on in the outside world. As a matter of fact, he doesn't even know what day it is!

The trainer keeps a log throughout the training period, recording what time the runner goes to bed, what time he wakes up, what he eats, and what he rejects. You see, the runner is striving for the mastery and therefore has to be temperate in all things. That temperance is to guide every area of his life.

Then the day of the race comes. The runner walks into the arena, unencumbered by all the weights he has worn in the past. And when the race begins, he starts running as free as the wind. Now he isn't running as fast as he did when he first started training. Now he's running *hot*, faster than he has ever run before — free from every weight and hindrance!

All of us must strive for a crown as well — the crown of fulfilling God's destiny on our lives. Hebrews 12:1 talks about the spiritual race we have to run to obtain that crown:

Therefore we also, since we are surrounded by so great a cloud of witnesses, let us lay aside every weight, and the sin which so easily ensnares us, and let us

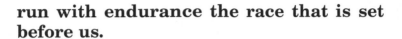

run with endurance the race that is set before us.

We are in the middle of a race God has set before us. As our divine Trainer, God is telling each and every one of us that it's time to unstrap all those weights that have hindered us for so long. We are to lay aside every weight and every sin that keeps us from obtaining the crown at the end of the race.

The word "therefore" in verse 1 points us back to Hebrews 11, where the Bible talks about our great "cloud of witnesses" — all the masters of the faith who have come before us and are now surrounding us in Heaven's grandstands, cheering us on as we run our race. They know what it is like to want to give up and quit. But they never quit in the middle of *their* race, and now they're yelling out encouragement to us: "Keep going! Don't quit! You'll make it! You can win the prize!"

That great cloud of witnesses is right — you *can* win the prize if you do what your Trainer has told you to do. Lay aside every weight and the sin that so easily besets you. Lay aside every wrong thought, every negative word, every bad habit. And if the believers you've been hanging around with have been hindering you in your race, lay aside your associations as well! Free yourself of every encumbrance, and determine never to quit. You have a race to run and a prize to obtain! You're striving for the mastery!

I guarantee you this: Should you ever begin to slack off in your walk with God, it will eventually show up. It may not show up today or next week, but sooner or later, it will be obvious to all when you fail to obtain the crown God has set before you.

When I was involved in sports as a boy, I remember one of my greatest problems was that I had natural talent. You see, I never had to work at it. I never had to train. I could drink Cokes and eat chocolate bon bons while the other guys were sweating and working out. Then I'd just go right out and do what I needed to do. But do you know what? My ability to do that eventually came to an end!

Natural talent comes to an end for all of us. In the final analysis, the one who wins the race is the one who is temperate in all things and *strives for the mastery*!

Now let's go back to what Paul said in Second Corinthians 9:26 (*KJV*):

I therefore so run, not as uncertainly; so fight I, not as one that beateth the air.

Paul said he ran "not as uncertainly." In other words, he had a specific goal and purpose for training so hard — he wanted to win his prize! And that goal didn't change when it was time to get into the "boxing ring" of life. That's why Paul said he fought "not as one that beats the air."

Paul is alluding here to this same runner who strives for the mastery in an Olympian foot race. Only this time, the athlete is getting in a boxing ring to fight.

However, even though this person may be strong in running, he *isn't* necessarily strong in boxing. That means he can't let down in this area of his life; he still has to strive for the mastery. Otherwise, when he finally gets into the ring with his opponent and begins to box, he will only be able to stay in the fight for two or three rounds before he starts taking wild swings. He'll swing and swing, but he won't be able to hit his opponent.

My friend, let me explain something to you about your "boxing match" with the devil. The devil isn't playing by decision — he plays for keeps! He is going to stay in the fight with you until you knock him out or he knocks you out. Take your pick — it's one or the other.

Satan will chase you down. You'll want to get away, saying, "Leave me alone! Leave me alone!" But he'll just say, "No way! Are you kidding? I want to win this match!"

That's just the way the devil operates against us. But understand this: Satan cannot *destroy* us; he can only *distract* us. Knowing this, Paul says, "I don't fight as one who beats the air — I have a goal in my swing! That's why I'm very serious about my training. I am temperate in all things, always putting my body under."

Now, the word "beat" in this verse means *to strike under the eye*.[26] In fact, it carries the meaning of getting beaten up until you're black and blue!

---

[26] Reinecker and Rogers, p. 417.

Paul is saying, "I'll stick in there even when I'm getting struck black and blue from all directions. It doesn't matter to me. I bring my body into subjection and make it my slave. My body serves *me*; I don't serve *it*. My mind serves me; I don't serve my mind."

Paul finishes by explaining why he keeps his body under: **"...lest that by any means, when I have preached to others, I myself should be a castaway"** (v. 27).

That word "castaway" is the Greek word *adokimos*, translated "reprobate" in other New Testament scriptures. This word tells us that unless we stick to the Word of God — unless we strive for the mastery and are temperate in all things — we ourselves will be disqualified for the prize and found to be useless in this life.

Be honest with yourself for just a moment. Have you ever preached the truth to others when you weren't even acting on your own words? More than likely, you have to answer yes to that question. However, that is a dangerous spiritual state to remain in if you don't want to be disqualified in the spiritual race God has given you to run!

So strive for the mastery every minute of the day. Don't give up. Don't quit just because the devil tries to chase you down and give you a black eye. That's nothing to be surprised about. After all, he is the devil; he isn't going to just roll over and quit!

It doesn't matter whether or not your eyes get black and blue from all the hits you're taking. Give

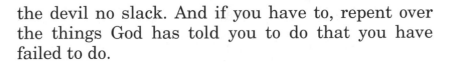

the devil no slack. And if you have to, repent over the things God has told you to do that you have failed to do.

Satan can accuse you regarding the Word you hear but fail to act upon, but that doesn't mean you shouldn't hear the Word anymore! It just means you must start striving for the mastery if you want to fulfill the destiny God has ordained for you. You have to lay aside every weight, stay with the Word of God, and then run with diligence and discipline the race God has set before you! And as you run your race, always remember this truth: Satan cannot schedule your *destruction* — he can only schedule your *distraction*.

Stick With the Word

Let me emphasize this point one more time: In order to conquer your mind, my friend, you *must* stick with the Word of God. Regardless of what anyone else thinks or says, that Word has to become everything to you, day in and day out, day in and day out, day in and day out.

You see, God is so full of love and mercy that He didn't want you to have to figure everything out on your own. So He wrote you a Book and told you, "This is now who you are." You don't have to meditate on or confess God's Word to try to obtain something from Him. You meditate on the Word because it is true. You're not working to receive something from God, because He has already given you everything you need for life and godliness!

So utilize the scriptural strategies God gives you in His Word to conquer your mind:

- Let God be true and every man a liar in every situation of life.

- Let the peace of God rule in your heart as a divine umpire, helping you decide the right way to go.

- Let no corrupt communication that produces death instead of life come out of your mouth.

- Let yourself not grow weary as you strive for the mastery and run your spiritual race.

- Let not sin reign as king in your life; instead, present your mind and your body as instruments of righteousness unto the Lord.

- Examine yourself on a regular basis, making sure you are walking in line with the Word in every area of your life.

- Keep in mind that Satan cannot destroy you; he can only *distract* you.

And never forget — the day you received Jesus Christ as the Lord of your life is the day you died. Everything negative you ever thought about yourself; all those death-dealing words that were spoken to you as a child; all the hurts and offenses you suffered; all the bad habits that controlled you — *all* of that died the day you received Jesus. You were given a brand-new identity. You were given a new family. You were given a new *you*.

Whenever a thought tells you anything contrary to that, just remember that the enemy is trying to steal from you what it already yours. You are healed, and someone is trying to steal your health. You are prosperous, and someone is trying to steal your money. You have a blessed marriage, and someone is trying to steal your marital happiness!

Personally, I don't care what thoughts run through my mind. I am only interested in what God's Word says. God's Word is the only source I allow to give me my thoughts. If someone asks me, "Well, what do you think?" I just say, "Let me look in the Word!"

That's why I can say that everything about my life is absolutely perfect. I'm not saying my life is perfect because I see perfection with my natural eyes. I'm saying that it's perfect because that is what God says belongs to me.

I don't have to work to try to make my life right because God has given me a new covenant. In this covenant, He promises that He will remember my sins and iniquities no more. As far as God is concerned, my sins do not exist — and neither do yours!

God has made you righteous. He has given you the ability to stand in His presence without the sense of guilt, as if sin never existed. That means any sense of guilt or failure you could ever feel never comes from Him. In His eyes, you are complete in Jesus. You are seated with Christ in heavenly places, looking *down* on all the principalities and powers who are trying to defeat you!

That is the truth about you, friend! That is the reality you can continually live in, day by day and moment by moment. And it all starts with taking control of your mind.

Outside of God's Word, no one's opinion means anything — not yours, not the world's, and certainly not the devil's. That's why you must stick with the Word at all costs. Never let yourself give up in your quest to take control of your mind and live according to God's truth about *you*!

Prayer for the Restoration of Your Mind

Perhaps you have been struggling to gain control of your mind, longing to live in the freedom Jesus purchased for you. If you would like to begin renovating your mind right now according to the Word of God, please pray this prayer from your heart:

Heavenly Father, I confess to You right now
that I have allowed other things in my life
to become more important to me than Your Word.
I have allowed wrong thoughts to rule in my mind
and drive me into actions that caused me
to walk away from You.

I thank You that I am forgiven
and that You are cleansing me right now
by the blood of Jesus.
I also thank You that Your power drives
those thoughts from my mind
as I choose to think right, speak right, and do right
according to Your Word.

From this moment forward,
it is my decision not to allow wrong thoughts
to reign in my mind any longer.
I will no longer act on the sins or the hurts of my past.
I choose to act only on that which is written
until the Word is a living reality in my life.
In Jesus' Name, amen.

FOR FURTHER INFORMATION

For additional copies of this book,
for further information
regarding Robb Thompson's ministry schedule,
or for a complete listing of Robb Thompson's
books, audiotapes, and videotapes,
please write or call:

**Family Harvest Church
18500 92nd Ave.
Tinley Park, IL 60477
1-877-WIN-LIFE
(1-877-946-5433)**

ABOUT THE AUTHOR

For more than a decade, Robb Thompson has pastored the congregation of Family Harvest Church in Tinley Park, Illinois, reaching out to the Chicago area with a practical, easily understood message of hope. A hallmark of his exciting ministry has been his ability to teach Christians how to act on God's Word and move out in faith so they can become *winners* in this life. Today, Robb Thompson's teaching ministry continues to grow through books, tapes, and the ever-expanding television program, *Winning in Life*, as he ministers to people throughout the United States and around the world.